A VOICE FOR REFORM...

MONSIGNOR STEPHEN J. KELLEHER holds a Doctorate in Canon Law from Catholic University in Washington, D.C., and was a member of the Marriage Tribunal of the Archdiocese of New York from 1943 to 1968, serving as its presiding judge for the last seven of those years. Through his various positions on the Tribunal, he gained vast experience in marriage counseling and related areas. In September 1968 he wrote an article advocating the abolition of the tribunal as well as the acceptance of divorce and remarriage within the Catholic Church. Shortly thereafter, he was removed as head of the Tribunal.

In *Divorce and Remarriage for Catholics?* Monsignor Kelleher sets forth the reasons which led him to that position and calls on the Church to recognize and act on their validity. His basic thesis is that when a marriage becomes "intolerable," and attempts to restore it have failed, then each partner ought to be able to find relief from it without threat of exclusion from the religious community and especially the sacramental life of the Church. As he states in the *Foreword:* "A Christian man and a woman who have suffered through a marriage that actually never was a marriage, or that was a marriage but painfully died, have a right to divorce, to marry a second time and to remain in full communion with the Christian community as well as the civil community.... A second marriage may be the only opportunity for a new life, an opportunity for the man and woman to rise and grow again."

Since its publication, this work has stimulated extensive discussion within Catholic circles and among the hierarchy, evoking increasing cries for reevaluation of the Church's traditional position regarding marriage and divorce. It is, in sum, a most timely and relevant book: a compassionate plea for reform where it is so urgently needed.

DIVORCE AND REMARRIAGE FOR CATHOLICS?

Stephen J. Kelleher

IMAGE BOOKS

A DIVISION OF DOUBLEDAY & COMPANY, INC.
GARDEN CITY, NEW YORK

This book is dedicated to my father and my mother, as well as to the rest of my family which includes the friends with whom I am blessed and have been blessed over the years. Whatever good comes to the reader through this book is the result of the help I have received from all the members of my family to be myself, speak myself and write myself.

The faults and mistakes in the book are my own. Each of us is responsible for his own mistakes.

Image Books Edition
published by special arrangement
with Doubleday & Company, Inc.
Image Books Edition February 1976

Portions of the Epilogue
originally appeared in *National Catholic Reporter*.

Copyright © 1973, 1976 by Stephen J. Kelleher
All Rights Reserved
PRINTED IN THE UNITED STATES OF AMERICA

Contents

	Foreword	6
I.	What Is the Problem?	12
II.	Marriage and Divorce in Scripture	31
III.	Marriage and Divorce in Theology	42
IV.	The Meaning of Marriage	58
V.	The Perfection of Marriage	69
VI.	Preparation for and Perseverance in Marriage	76
VII.	The Importance of Good Marriage Laws	84
VIII.	The Intolerable Marriage and the Tribunal	91
IX.	Inside the Tribunal	104
X.	Reasons for Divorce and Annulment in Church Law	117
XI.	Basic Incompatibility Is the Only Reason for Dissolution	131
XII.	A Search for Change	137
XIII.	The Good Conscience Solution	144
XIV.	Second Marriage and Full Membership	150
	Epilogue	157

Foreword

A Christian man and a woman who have suffered through a marriage that actually never was a marriage, or that was a marriage but painfully died, have a right to divorce, to marry a second time and to remain in full communion with the Christian community as well as the civil community. This right to marry a second time may even be more demanding than the right to marry a first time because of the already awakened sense of the need these individuals have for the abiding love and affection of a healthy marriage.

Every Catholic, equally, has a right to and a need for Holy Communion. All have a need to participate actively in the Eucharistic celebration, the central act of worship in the Catholic Church and the effective sign of unity with Christ. They have a right to be welcomed with open arms into the Catholic community and to participate fully in the activities of that community. The right of a Catholic to marry a second time should also carry with it his right to participate actively in the Eucharistic celebration by receiving Holy Communion.

Just as his right to marry a second time may be more pressing than his right to marry the first time, so his right to and need for Holy Communion in the Eucharistic celebration may be spiritually and emotionally more necessary in his second marriage. The frustration of an intolerable first marriage will have created the need for openly compassionate help from Christ and from His Church if his second marriage is to be a joyful sharing with his wife in the whole Christ, the Nazareth and Risen Christ as well as the Suffering and Dying Christ.

Many Orthodox, Protestants and other Christians who are not Catholic, will be able to apply to themselves the substantial content of this position without difficulty or scruple. There are basic contradictions between the beliefs of Christian communities and the beliefs of other religious communities; but, despite these contradictions, members of the Jewish and Moslem communities, and members of other religious communities that are not Christian will be able to see the underlying values of the position in the context of their own centuries old religious traditions.

Persons of any or no religion may find that the following values, these basic human truths, apply equally to all men and all women. Once a man is born he is intended to grow. As an adult he ordinarily grows best in loving union with a woman. Ordinarily, the love and life of both grow and blossom in marriage. A sick marriage stunts growth and dries up marital love. When a marriage becomes intolerably sick, it diminishes more and more the potential growth and dignity of the man and the woman no matter how much they strive to remain alive and grow. When, in spite of genuine attempts to cure the ills, the marriage dies, divorce is a necessity. A second marriage may be the only opportunity for a new life, an opportunity for the man and the woman to rise and grow again.

This book will be concerned in large part with the rights of Catholics in intolerable marriages to divorce and marry a second time and with the right of these persons to be warmly received into the Catholic community. Further, it will propose that their condition be accepted in ecclesiastical law without judgment by the Church. This latter point would in effect abolish the marriage tribunals in the Church which now pass judgment on the condition of marriages regarding their validity, nullity and dissolution. My reasons for this, to many, drastic reform in Catholic attitude and practice toward divorce, remarriage and tribunal judgment will be presented and discussed in the chapters to come.

My views in these matters were developed principally from my experience with men and women whose marriages never truly existed or had died because their relationship had become intolerable. My experience derived from my working with the matrimonial tribunals in the United States and in Rome and from my observations of the workings of these tribunals in Canada, England, the South American countries and the Middle East. In a way, I owe this book to those people who could not find justice in the tribunals of the Church, but, in truth, it was a long time in coming. I was involved in tribunal work, with the exception of 1960 and 1961, from 1943 to 1968. For the last six of those years I was the presiding judge in the tribunal of the Archdiocese of New York.

In thinking back now of those who are responsible for this book, I remember vividly, and painfully, the anguished faces of many of the thousands of persons, individuals and couples, with whom I have spoken in the New York tribunal as well as in the parish houses, private homes and in the streets of the Archdiocese of New York about the problems in their marriages. Sometimes the faces showed deep anguish, but frequently there was hostility, fear, confusion. Now and again there was hate. Worst of all, there was, at times, no sign of feeling.

These persons, these couples, had one thought in mind. They wanted the Church (and, for them, I and others in tribunal work were the Church) to declare that they were free from an utterly impossible and "dead" marriage so that they might remarry or have a second marriage recognized by the Church and continue to go to Holy Communion. They wanted so much to be warmly welcomed as full members of the Church.

In the early years of my tribunal work I sensed little of the anguish of persons in intolerable marriages. I felt perplexed rather than pained. It is with deep regret that I recall I sometimes responded to hostility with hostility, to coldness with coldness. It took me a long time to realize that the reticence often displayed by seekers of annulments or divorces was generated, at least in part, by my legalistic and attemptedly objective approach to their problems. This reticence was accompanied by and may have been the cause of their inability to communicate with clarity the nub of the problem that had made their marriage initially or subsequently intolerable. In almost every instance, the intolerability of their marriage had made them destructive of themselves and each other. They had become destructive of their children.

Over the years, I began to question the anonymity—the

impersonality—of the whole procedure. I recall one person shouting at one of the priests, "The trouble with you, Father, is that you are too goddam pompous." It might have been said to any one of us. I remember one man who was surprised to find that I had been the principal person in helping him obtain an annulment. He thought I was the prosecuting attorney in his case. I remember another instance where a person literally hated the presiding judge although it was this particular judge who had successfully and somewhat ingeniously gathered the evidence so that the marriage was annulled.

With time and experience, mellowed with more personal compassion, I made more creative attempts in the use of jurisprudence to assist people in intolerable first marriages or those in "bad" second marriages. Even then it was apparent that the procedures themselves were unjust and lacked a modicum of the compassion which should be a basic sign of the Church of Christ. The next logical step in the pursuit of justice in the adjudication of marriage cases was, obviously, to reform the juridical procedures. This route was tried, frequently thwarted, partially successful; but it became apparent that even attempts to reform the procedures would ultimately have to end in failure, because the basic difficulty was the substantive law itself. Procedural reform from within would not reach the root of the problem. As I shall try to demonstrate, the juridical structure is inherently artificial and unreal. The marriage tribunal is not a viable approach to the problem of the intolerable marriage. But, the mentality within the Church legal system is simply incapable of conceiving that the system itself is useless and that the best possible reform would be its complete abolition.

My suggestion that the marriage tribunals be abolished (*America*, September 14, 1968) brought a reaction that shows how difficult it is for many churchmen to think beyond the boundaries of the narrow legal structures that confine their minds. One reader's response was that I was denying the doctrine of the indissolubility of marriage. This was obviously meant to imply that suggesting the abolition of the tribunal was heresy. For not a few that would be true. Most priests were not so absurd as to scream "heresy," but many were shocked at the idea. The fact is that for many canonists, lawyers, bishops, tribunal judges of a large number of dioceses, and for the members of the Roman Rota and the curia and, I dare say, for the pope himself, the present law is an unquestionable protector of doctrine and morals and a domain which itself is neat and clean and quite well adapted to dispense justice to the peoples of the world with but a few adjustments in procedures and a few concessions to due process. Stepping mentally outside the quiet, sterile, paneled, judicial enclave of doctrinal security and moral righteousness into the real world of "the other" people, I found the halls of justice in shambles and the legal structure of the Church in decay.

And looking to scripture scholars, patrologists, theologians, historians, civil lawyers, doctors, psychiatrists, psychologists and sociologists I found no reason to support the body of matrimonial law as enshrined in the Code of Canon Law; no need to uphold the structure of the marriage tribunals; and no excuse for imposing its procedures on the people of God.

This book is not a treatise on all the converging evidence for assuming this position. Neither is it an account of the personal evolution of my thought through the chronology of experience briefly outlined here, but I trust it will be an ordered presentation of the position I have arrived at through my tribunal experience, through thoughtful consideration of the problems and areas of possible solutions, through my own research and the assistance of many friends who are considerable scholars in fields other than my own. In some measure, all of these elements will be found on every page.

It will be a practical book based on practical experience. It is my fervent wish that the book may awaken in the minds of those in authority at least the urgency of the need for radical change in the provisions of the Code of Canon Law to deal effectively and realistically with a problem so fraught with despair and frustration for so many. It is also my devout prayer that what is said here may give to those who have been burdened with marital problems, rather than blessed with marital peace, not only some hope for future relief, but some comfort and help in the present resolution of their anxiety.

Foreword

In formulating my position as expressed in this book, I owe a great debt of gratitude to Mr. Anthony Lee. He was particularly helpful in relating the great gap that exists between the prescriptions of canon law and its practices regarding marriage on one hand and the sacramentality of matrimony on the other, which is a major theological contribution to this volume. Further, Mr. Lee proved to be not only an able theologian in this and other areas of the exposition but an astute editor of the entire manuscript and a severe critic of this canon lawyer, in particular. It is simply the truth that this book would not have been written without his help.

It is just as true that this book would not even have been attempted without the graciously insistent persuasion of Doctor Jose M. Chaves and the strong guidance of John L. Springer. To each of these three good friends I am deeply grateful.

I am also grateful to John J. Delaney, the religion editor of Doubleday & Company, Inc., and the members of his staff for their relaxed, helpful and encouraging assistance. They made it easy for me to write my first book.

I

What Is the Problem?

The problem is one of injustice—the injustice of the marriage law of the Roman Catholic Church, the injustice in the juridical processes of its marriage courts, and the injustice in the judgments of diocesan tribunals and in the decisions of the Roman Rota and the other tribunals in Rome. Every Catholic who has suffered an intolerable marriage and has submitted his or her case to the judicial system of the Church for adjudication, or who has sought spiritual relief in a "bad" marriage has in some measure suffered injustice at the hands of the Church, whatever the final outcome of the case. Some sincere members of the clergy who have worked hard in the marriage tribunals of the Church for the good of souls will consider this a gross exaggeration. If anything, it is an understatement of the problem.

If the unity of the people of God is such that if "anyone is honored, all rejoice therein" and "if anyone suffers anything, all in some measure suffer," then the truth is that every Catholic suffers a certain injustice because of the Church's matrimonial laws and practices. This is indeed a sweeping indictment. Initial indications of the truth of the allegation are the common misconceptions of Catholics about the nature of marriage, in general, and about the law and practices of the Church regarding marriage in particular. No law is just that is imposed on a community without being promulgated in such a way that the members of the community, at least for the most part, understand the terms and the consequences of the law. Church law is sometimes couched in language that deceives the masses of the people it governs. Its legal procedures and judgments are often kept secret from the public in cases that arise from public cause and will have public effect, and this is particularly true of cases involving annulments

What Is the Problem?

and divorces. Such secrecy is manifestly unjust to all the people. These facts do not impugn malice with regard to the Church, its legislators, its offices or its courts. They do indicate that the mass of matrimonial legislation—accumulated over the centuries and codified into the present body of Canon Law in 1918—and the juridical procedures, which reflect a mixture of old Roman law and the confidentiality of confessional secrecy, do not do justice to the people of the Church today. To say that the matrimonial legislation of the present Code of Canon Law is foreign to the American concept of justice (which has been said repeatedly by any number of Americans and by the Canon Law Society of America) is not enough; it is "foreign" to our world and to our time.

This will become clearer if we compare the common understanding of the Catholic layman regarding the teaching of the Church on marriage and his sense of justice with the actual doctrine of the Church and its juridical practices.

*

For the most part, Catholics believe that it is an infallible teaching of the Church that divorce and remarriage is absolutely forbidden and that this teaching is based on Sacred Scripture. Almost all Catholics are familiar with one passage or another that confirms that belief; e.g., the easier of memory is probably, "Let no man separate what God has joined." (Matthew 19:6.) Most Catholics know that there is such a thing as annulment and that this can happen to a Catholic couple. When it does, both parties are free to marry because there never was a marriage in the first place. So that doesn't disturb the doctrine of indissolubility.

Some Catholics know a little about certain isolated impediments, as "first cousins can't marry" or "you can't marry a non-Catholic without a dispensation." But unless there is personal involvement most Catholics don't know about such intricacies as the difference between dispensations of mixed religion and of disparity of cult, or the impediments of affinity and spiritual relationship, not to mention error, force and fear, abduction, physical impotency, lack of form, existing bond, age, vows, crime, legal relationship or public propriety—any of which are grounds for annulment. Even fewer know there are other grounds for annulment such as simulation, lack of due discretion and psychic impotence.

Someplace along the line, perhaps at a cocktail party or a gossip session, a Catholic layman "in the know" might have shrugged off one of those "scandalous marriages of a Hollywood divorcee to a Catholic, by a priest, in the Church" with the comment that it was allowed by reason of the Pauline or Petrine Privilege. Most laymen would not understand that, and a number would continue to think "When you've got money . . . well, see for yourself." On the average, however, Catholic laymen do not become embroiled in tribunal processes, and they take it for granted that those few who do are treated with justice and mercy as befits the case.

For those many, many Catholics who understand the teaching and practice of the Church approximately as outlined above and then suffer a breakdown in their own marriage, the world of ecclesiastical law and juridical practice comes as a terrible shock to their faith, a blow to their dignity and, more often than not, a violation of justice to their cause. Given cause and reason to investigate the teaching of the Church, and given the experience of the juridical procedures, they find the truth is not what they were led to believe and that the justice of the Church is of another kind.

※

While it is obviously the teaching of the Roman Catholic Church that marriage is indissoluble, this teaching is not *de fide;* i.e., it is not an infallible teaching and has never been defined by the Church as a doctrine of Faith. The Bible does not unconditionally confirm that teaching. Further, the Fathers of the Church are not unanimous, and the history of Church practice is not consistent on the subject. In fact, historically, the practice in many parts of the Church permitted divorce and remarriage, and this practice was based on direct appeal to the teaching of Sacred Scripture and the Fathers and, if not sanctioned, was at least tolerated by some popes and councils of the Church during the first millennium. Further, even in the practice of the Roman Catholic Church under the present Code of Canon Law the term "indissolubility" admits of a number of distinctions and, in fact, the

What Is the Problem?

Church does dissolve valid, non-sacramental, consummated marriages under certain conditions "in favor of the Faith," and it does dissolve valid, sacramental, Christian and Catholic marriages that are not consummated. In these instances, the Church not only acknowledges, but grants divorces.

If these facts offend the sensibilities of some Catholic laymen who believe that the Church has always taught the absolute indissolubility of marriage, even more do they offend the acumen of many scholars in scripture, patrology, theology and history who are convinced that the Church has assumed an indefensible posture on the subject of Christian marriage in its legislation. Some of the opinions of scholars regarding the significance of the "indissolubility of marriage" in the history of theological development and in the practice of the Church in the East and West will be discussed in subsequent chapters. Here it would be well to complete the comparison between the Catholic layman's usual sense of justice and the justice of the matrimonial laws of the Church.

*

The average American layman's expectation of justice includes such basic legal concepts as the following: anyone making a petition to a court will receive a hearing before an unbiased judge or tribunal; evidence to the contrary will be open to review; and witnesses to the contrary can be cross-examined by the claimant's counsel. In a criminal charge, the accused not only receives these advantages of due process, but certain presumptions of the law in favor of the accused; e.g., the accused is innocent before the law until proved guilty before the court. In criminal matters, such as a felony, the judgment is made by a panel of jurors, peers of the accused, under the watchful supervision of a judge who guarantees that the rules of due process, the admittance of evidence and the examination of witnesses are carried out without prejudice to the accused. Any watcher of American T.V. in general, and "Perry Mason," "The Defenders," "The Bold Ones" or "Owen Marshall, Counselor at Law," in particular, knows that the prosecuting attorney represents the state in the criminal trial. It is also general knowledge that the prosecuting attorney must abide by the same rules of due process, the same legal presumption of innocence, the same rules of admittance of evidence and cross examination of witnesses as the counsel of defense. No one is foolish enough to expect that because of these safeguards there are not some cases of miscarriage of justice, but again there are courts of appeal in case of an unfavorable judgment. At the same time there is the protection from double jeopardy, which prohibits the accused in a criminal trial being subjected to a second trial once a judgment has been delivered in his favor. And there is a statute of limitations protecting against a person being indicted for an unresolved crime of the distant past. This is not a claim that the civil court system is flawless or that its performance is always efficient. In fact, in many quarters there are complaints about the abuses of the system and the backlog of cases to be adjudicated. Even though this system is not perfect, it represents a serious attempt in the presumptions of the law, in the rules of due process to administer justice in an honest and equitable manner for the common good of society and in accord with the rights, honor and dignity of the individual.

The practicing lawyer will be aware of many other refinements of due process, of legal fictions, and procedural technicalities which can be utilized in various levels of hearings and trials. The important point here is that the law with all its refinements and intricacies is intended for the benefit of the individual person in an ordered society of men. When the law or the procedures fail in that endeavor, the laws can be changed and new procedures and precedents can be introduced into the jurisprudence which will, in a continuing dynamic, adjust to the conditions of the society the law benefits.

※

The law of the Church, and the matrimonial law in particular, falls far short of the most rudimentary expectation of justice of the ordinary citizen. To make an exhaustive list of particulars is hardly necessary at this point when a few broad categories at the very foundation of the matrimonial law yield enough examples to show that the "justice" administered under the law is unrealistic, arbitrary, lacking in due

What Is the Problem?

process, and contrary to human dignity and the basic rights of the individual.

It is important to note that the problems to be discussed are all intrinsic to the law; the claim is not that grave injustice is being done to Catholics because of administrative deficiencies—not enough courts, not enough personnel to man the courts, interminable delays, indecision and uncertainty in handling certain cases, and the other frustrations common to many bureaucratic and institutional administrations. All of these are true in some measure in various places throughout the world. Under discussion here is the basic, universal law itself.

*

Central to the entire body of matrimonial law is a host of theological presumptions. Many of these presumptions are being questioned by scholars today and some pertinent ones will be discussed later. Here we stress a legal presumption which permeates the entire legal procedure within the law. In contrast to the presumption of the civil law in the United States that the accused party is innocent until proven guilty, it is the very strong presumption of the matrimonial law of the Church that in all cases the bond of marriage is presumed to be valid unless otherwise proved. The position was advanced by Pope Innocent III who lived at the beginning of the thirteenth century. The theological implications are not at issue here; rather, the practice. From the time of Pope Innocent III, in any doubtful cases regarding the existence of the marriage bond, judgment must be made "in favor of matrimony."

This presumption of the law was further strengthened by Pope Benedict XIV in a Papal Bull issued on November 3, 1741, entitled *Dei miseratione,* from the opening words, "By the mercy of God." The bull instructed that each diocese, the tribunal in Rome called the "Roman Rota," and the Congregation of the Holy Office should have a "Defender of the Bond" chosen for his legal skill and moral integrity. He was to uphold the presumption that the marriage bond was existing and valid in every case brought before the respective tribunal. He was to oversee the examination of witnesses, to defend the bond orally and in writing, and his position had "to be cited in every judicial act" of the process. Further, if a decision of the nullity of a marriage should be handed down by the tribunal, the decision would have to be appealed by the defender of the bond to another court or to Rome for another decision in favor of the bond. Two decisions by different courts were required by law to declare a marriage null, no matter how clear the evidence. And if the defender of the bond could produce new evidence even after two decisions in favor of the petitioner, the defender was bound to open the case again against the petitioner; i.e., in favor of the bond. A marriage procedure was never to be a *res judicata*—a closed case. Double jeopardy, even the possibility of triple jeopardy, is positively included and stressed in Church law.

Some scholars have seen at the root of this legislation another presumption of law—the presumption that the petitioner is to be suspected of dishonesty when approaching the Church for an annulment. John T. Noonan, Jr., says, "To anticipate evasion, to forestall corruption, collusion and connivance, to discourage negligence, Benedict XIV recollected what he had learned as Prospero Lambertini and constructed a set of rules to rationalize, channel, and control the [marriage tribunal] process." (*Power to Dissolve—Lawyers and Marriages in the Courts of the Roman Curia*, Harvard University Press, Cambridge, Mass., 1972, p. 128.)

The presumption of the validity of every marriage and the role of the defender of the bond were incorporated in the Code of Canon Law that presently governs the universal Church. To count the 420 regulations of the Code governing the procedures for the annulment of marriage is to number the ways in which the validity, even of a doubtful bond, is protected by the Church law, for every prescription is based on that presumption.

There is an unfortunate similarity between the roles of the prosecuting attorney of the civil court and the defender of the bond of the Church marriage court. By reason of the rights and duties of the defender of the bond, the following presumptions arise in the Church marriage court: 1) the petitioner in a marriage case is treated as an accused criminal;

2) the accused is guilty until proven innocent; 3) the "marriage" is somehow the victim of the crime allegedly committed by the accused.

Given the fact that the law and the court is stacked against the petitioner, there can be little expectation of "due process" in the normal sense.

※

Canon law evidences a completely different approach to due process from the American idea of justice in a court of law. By way of comparison take the example of a case of murder—the State vs. Mr. Joe Jones for the murder of Cleopatra Jones. The prosecuting attorney represents the state in a legal action taken against Mr. Jones. The presumption of the law is that he is innocent until the prosecuting attorney can produce sufficient testimony of witnesses, admissible evidence and convincing arguments to prove to the jury without reasonable doubt that Mr. Jones actually committed the murder. The prosecuting attorney, however, is governed by the same rules of examination of witness, admission of evidence, cross examination as the counsel who defends Mr. Jones.

Now let us enter a marriage court in which Mr. Jones is petitioning for an annulment of his marriage with Cleopatra Jones on the grounds that when the marriage was performed Cleopatra had the intention of excluding children. In the marriage court it would line up like this—"The Church vs. Mr. Jones on the grounds that his marriage to Cleopatra is valid." The "defender of the bond" represents the Church in the interest of the victim "marriage." The presumption is that Mr. Jones is wrong until he proves beyond doubt that he is right. Further, the presumption of the law is that the words spoken by Cleopatra at the wedding represent true internal consent to have children until demonstrated otherwise.

The fact that she has constantly taken contraceptive pills since the wedding does not demonstrate an internal intention to exclude children at the time of the wedding, and the burden of proof is on Mr. Jones. Cleopatra is hostile to the action and refuses to give testimony. If through other witnesses (e.g., Cleopatra's roommate in college) it can be determined that she had before the marriage expressed her intention of never having children, and the decision of the tribunal would be in favor of nullity, the defender of the bond would have to appeal the case. Even after a second favorable decision, the defender could reopen the case if Cleopatra came forward to testify that she had no such intention, even though that might be a lie in order to block the nullity decision or to prevent Mr. Jones from remarrying.

The strange thing here is that the person who approached the Church for the resolution of the problem of an unhappy marriage can be frustrated in the name of preserving the dignity of the sacrament, while the person who in this case violated the object of matrimony by preventing conception can use the presumptions of the law vindictively to further degrade marriage and to undermine respect for the law and confidence in its procedures.

This is not an actual case, but it could be because the terms are built directly into the juridical procedures. It points up the almost complete disregard for due process, as we understand it.

- The presumptions of the law are against the petitioner.
- The court is itself hostile in appointing a defender of the bond.
- The defender of the bond (prosecutor) is given privilege in the process.
- The petitioner must prove his claim beyond a doubt.
- A favorable decision is not only subject to appeal, but must be appealed.
- Two favorable decisions are required.
- The case is never closed in favor of the petitioner.

※

Without going into the background for the distinctions, there are two kinds of valid marriages which can be "dissolved" according to Church law. The Church does dissolve valid marriages in which either or both members of the union is not baptized because such a union is not sacramental. The other kind of valid marriage that can be dissolved is the sacramental union of two baptized persons, whose marriage has not been physically consummated.

What Is the Problem?

At first glance, one would hardly think of the Sacrament of Baptism or the act of carnal intercourse as mere technicalities. But when these acts become, in law, the determining factor in the absolute indissolubility of marriage, then the suspicion that, on occasion, they are mere technicalities and their effects are legal fictions can hardly be avoided. Take the case of a certain Mr. X whose parents allowed him to be baptized as an infant at the urging of a traveling preacher at a revival meeting. The parents had little or no religion, they never provided the child with any religious training and he was totally unaware that he had ever been baptized. In his late teens and early twenties he became involved in an unhappy marriage and obtained a civil divorce. Later, in another locality, he wished to marry a Catholic girl and took instructions. Here we pick up the case in the words of William W. Bassett, a professor of Canon Law at the Catholic University of America in Washington, D.C.

> The case was sent in and petition made for the dissolution of his previous bond in favor of the faith. Then it was discovered that both he and his former spouse had been baptized as infants. On the basis of contractual theory the validity of the marriage appears unquestionable. Since he was baptized, it is also said that his first marriage was automatically a sacrament, whether he knew or intended it or not. (*The Bond of Marriage*, edited by William W. Bassett, University of Notre Dame Press, Notre Dame, Indiana, 1968, p. 164.)

True, it was a marriage of two baptized persons, but neither party was aware that there had ever been a baptism, neither was taught any religion, neither had ever joined a church or had any conscious understanding of the sacrament; but the law says that these two people conferred on each other the Sacrament of Matrimony, and because it is a sacrament and the marriage was consummated, it cannot be dissolved, not even by the pope, not even in favor of the faith.

Now this means that the sacrament of marriage has some kind of magical power that works without the knowledge or intention of the recipients. This magical power effects a marvelous sacramental sign of Christ's love for the Church—which neither party ever heard of and could not have cared less about. This sacramental sign, in turn, confers upon the marriage an absolute indissolubility which reflects the inseparable unity of Christ and the Church. Either this or the sacramentality of the marriage is a legal fiction which is no more a factual reality than were the intentions of the parties to confer a sacrament. Yet the justifiably puzzled Mr. X cannot marry a second time because the law says his first marriage was a sacrament.

*

In the present law, the pope has the power to dissolve a valid, sacramental marriage that has not been consummated. If the couple, however, engage even in a single act of carnal intercourse, the marriage is rendered absolutely indissoluble by any power on earth. The justification for holding this position, at least in the law, is that a marriage even of a baptized couple which is a true and valid sacramental marriage is not complete or perfect until it has been consummated by an act which is apt to generate a child. This sounds logical and reasonable. The same logic and reason infers also that it is not the "validity" (i.e., the consent) or the "sacramentality" of matrimony which finally renders the marital union indissoluble, but the first act of intercourse. In adjudicating a petition the questions are never raised as to whether the act of intercourse was a human act; i.e., a fully willed act not under fear, duress, or under the influence of drugs or alcohol; the question is never raised as to whether the two persons were actually engaging in or, however awkwardly, trying to engage in an act of love. So it can further be inferred that it is simply the carnal act that consummates marriage and makes it forever indissoluble.

Now the choice of explanation must be 1) that the first act of carnal intercourse, whether with knowledge, intention, even consciousness or not, has some magical power that no other act of intercourse has to consummate and render a union indissoluble, or 2) that the consummation is itself a legal fiction; i.e., that given the physical act it is legally as-

What Is the Problem?

sumed that consummation has occurred and the marriage rendered indissoluble, whether or not there was any genuine attempt to confirm the marriage. If the second choice is correct, another difficulty arises. The law does not allow even so much as an investigation of the real issue; i.e., whether or not true consummation has actually taken place, and therefore that indissolubility has been effected. Rather, the whole investigation and the only evidence admissible revolves around whether the act of intercourse took place or not.

In both of the issues considered above—baptism and sacramentality, consummation and indissolubility—a *sign* of something is accepted by the law as the *reality*. Then the law says that because it is the actual reality, all avenues of recourse are closed to the petitioner. In the first case, the *fact of baptism* is a *sign* that the possibility of sacramentality exists, but the fact of baptism in infancy alone cannot effectively confer the sacrament of matrimony on a subsequent union. It opens the possibility of the persons rendering the union sacramental, but the possibility that it might be sacramental does not make it so. The same can be said for the act of intercourse following a wedding ceremony in which mutual consent was exchanged and mutual love promised. The *act of intercourse* may be a *sign* that the couple intend to confirm what was promised at the wedding, but the simple fact of engaging in one act of carnal copulation does not necessarily confirm the marriage. It might be nothing more than another episode in a long line of sexual conquests which will not end if the new bride doesn't completely satisfy the new groom.

If this seems to be stretching the imagination, take the case of the young Catholic boy and girl who had been neighborhood sweethearts. Their parents felt they were too young to marry and have children. The boy went into military service for a year and then the couple decided to be married before he went overseas. The wedding was arranged and took place on a military base before he left on a tour of duty. The marriage was not physically consummated. In the first eighteen months of foreign duty the young man became involved in a number of sexual affairs and made excuses that he would have to sign over for an extension of his tour. More sexual exploits followed before he finally came back to his wife. In the two years of foreign service, the boy had lost his faith and his faithfulness to his wife; but he returned home knowing that if his wife didn't satisfy him as much as his recent conquests, he could go about satisfying his passion without her. The wife suspected his unfaithfulness, given the circumstances, but welcomed him home with love. They engaged in intercourse, but in the very act of consummation the girl realized that her husband had radically changed from the man she had wed. It was a sad episode for the girl. She showed some resistance after his rather cruel mockery of her virginity, and an argument about his fidelity ensued. The husband insisted on his rights, and the consummation was to her shockingly violent. But she was now involved in a valid, sacramental, consummated marriage and she had no way of proving that her husband had no intention of being faithful to her. She refused to cohabit with her husband after the first torturous night until she sought advice of her pastor. She was told to return to her husband, that she was "acting precipitously." But when she let it be known she wasn't kidding, she was advised that because the marriage was consummated there was no recourse but to seek an annulment. However, "subsequent infidelity" (which was the case when the husband had gotten into those first affairs overseas) was not grounds for annulment. The husband was embarrassed by the fact that, upon returning home after two years overseas' service, his wife stayed with him but one night. He therefore emphatically denied any intention of unfaithfulness. Both families, anxious to see the marriage work out, pressured the girl to at least "give the marriage a try." After several weeks of tension and pressure and realizing that since she was told that all avenues of dissolution were closed and annulment was impossible on the present grounds, and that if she did not go back she would spend the rest of her life with no husband, no children and one miserable "night of love" to remember, she gave in. Two years after she had given consent in a wedding ceremony; two years in which her husband had changed his moral and religious attitudes, and she too had matured in her judgment of love, romance and marriage and in her desire for motherhood; after two years of waiting, one night of consummation

What Is the Problem? 25

and several weeks of pressure and tension, she hesitantly returned to "give the marriage a fair try."

Needless to say it didn't work out. The marriage was intolerable. After it had produced two children, more unfaithfulness and a full measure of hatred, a divorce had to be obtained by the woman for her own sake and for the sake of the children who were now old enough to see and understand the infidelity and hatred. The mother is now raising the children in relative peace. The case does not at this time involve any view to remarriage on her part, although the husband has remarried without concern for the law of the Church. Perhaps an ingenious canonist could now process an annulment if she ever makes a petition. Now, after the intolerable marriage has run its painful course, one might be able to prove "lack of due discretion" or some other grounds for annulment. The tragedy in this case is that, according to Church law, the very act of consummation which "completed and perfected" that marriage, which made it legally indissoluble and which threw any hope of relief from the bond back on an annulment procedure, was the same act which confirmed to the bride that this was not the person or the union to which she had consented two years previously.

The law holds that consent to the act of intercourse verifies the consent given in the marriage ceremony and that the act itself completes the sacrament conferred in the ceremony. I submit that the first is a presumption of the law and the second is a fiction of the law in the case just described. The reserved consent to the act of intercourse was not a verification of the total consent given in the marriage two years previously. And while the act of intercourse might generally be considered a *sign* that the parties wish to confirm what was promised in the wedding ceremony, it certainly wasn't in the case above, and the case lacked any other verifying sign.

I submit also that the suffering, the hatred, the "fatherless" children in this case are the result of unrealistic technicalities and fictions of the law, and that grave injustice was done in the name of preserving an "indissoluble" marriage.

Many other presumptions and fictions of the law in the present Code of Canon Law are unrealistic and unjust and, like those above, bring untold misery to thousands of Catholics in cases that will never be brought before the marriage tribunals. Such injustice and misery also brings harm to the Church as an institution and to the clergy and hierarchy. When injustice is "canonized" it spreads distrust for the very churchmen who in all sincerity try to make the law work for the good of the people. The problem is that the law itself is too often constructed not for the good of the people, but for the good of the institution. Pastors and priests at the parish level readily admit that they must struggle under the burden of canon law and, in fact, are compelled at times to operate in spite of, or in opposition to, some of the canons, in order to bring justice and mercy to their pastoral administration.

The same is true of the officials who administer the law itself in the tribunals and in the courts. In a number of dioceses the tendency has been to by-pass much of the canonical process, while still paying it lip service, in order to arrive at a pastoral solution. This is commendable in that it shows mercy and brings forth the spirit rather than the letter; it is valuable in that it dramatizes the inadequacy, unreality and injustice of the law; it is noteworthy in that this approach has been taken by bishops and priests of high rank in their tribunals.

In the October 10, 1971, issue of *America*, Father John Catoir, presiding judge of the tribunal in Paterson, New Jersey, described such a method of effecting a pastoral solution. The so-called pastoral solution, however, does not attack the root of the problem—the question of competency. There are two aspects of the question. Viewed from the position of the petitioner, the problem appears to be one of anonymity of the tribunal and the judges. Viewed from the tribunal bench, the question turns more on "who is competent to judge" in these cases.

※

There is an adage that gives a feeling of justice and security to most Americans, even when things seem to be going wrong, "You will have your day in court." When we feel we have a just cause we feel we will get a just hearing. There is a certain expectation that, no matter how fearful and trembling you might be standing before the court, you will have your chance face to face to present your case to your judge, that the judge will hear your case and understand it, and that he will give you his judgment and you will hear it and understand it. Even in a criminal court there is a certain clarity and finality, a certain justice and judgment when the judge, face to face with the convicted person, says, "Do you have any more to say before I pass sentence?"

Put briefly, men expect to be judged by their fellow men. They resent and resist being judged by a mechanical dispenser of documents, whether that be a government agency, an institution or a computer. The marriage tribunals under the present Code of Canon Law are so impersonal as to bring contempt on their judgments.

Few persons involved in a marriage appeal come to know personally even their own advocates; i.e., their own ecclesiastical attorneys who represent their case. The defender of the marriage bond is often an invisible, mysterious, hostile shadow who rarely, if ever, appears on the scene, but who is known to have passed on every word of testimony and written a defense against the petition. Ordinarily, there are three judges appointed to each case. The principals in the action and the witnesses, pro and con, usually only see one judge. The other judges will make their decisions without "hearing the case." They will base their decisions on the written briefs.

If the judgment should be favorable to the petitioner (i.e., the annulment granted) in the first court, which is usually in the diocese of the petitioner, the decision is appealed to another court in another diocese. At the second "trial" the parties to the marriage may never appear. They may never know or ever speak to their advocate in the appeal case. They will probably never know who were the judges. Should the appeals court reverse the first decision, the case goes to Rome for the determining judgment. Here the anonymity is even greater, and only very rarely is there any more involved than processing the documents prepared by the lower courts. Decisions are ground out which supersede all other local judgments. Months, perhaps years, have passed and the parties to the marriage have perhaps discussed their case with two officials of the tribunal—the advocate in the first trial and one judge who may have done no more than ask a list of questions prepared by the defender of the bond.

※

Closely related to the problem of anonymity is the problem of competency. Certain kinds of annulment cases can be processed at the diocesan level (as above described); a dissolution can be granted by a bishop in the case of a marriage of two unbaptized persons, if one of them becomes a Catholic. The Holy Father can dissolve non-sacramental marriages in favor of the faith and sacramental marriages that have not been consummated. In the law then, there is a hierarchy of competency to annul and dissolve marriages. As the grade goes up in competency to act on difficult cases, the more remote the decision maker is from the principals whose case he must judge.

The fact that a bishop is more anonymous to an individual case does not make him a more objective judge of the issues involved in the case. Just the opposite is true. The very fact that the bishop has more responsibility and more authority, because he is the first shepherd of the whole flock of an entire locality, makes him less apt to hear the individual petitions and make personal judgment regarding the disposition of individual cases. The cases reserved to the Holy Father and the cases submitted to the Roman courts from the United States and from all parts of the world are not more objectively judged than the cases in the New York Archdiocesan tribunal. Such lofty titles as the Sacred Roman Rota and the Supreme Sacred Signature (two tribunals in Rome) add nothing to the value of the decisions in annulment cases. They tend to add a mystical and magical note to the proceedings, but they do not improve the judicial quality of the judgments. In our times these titles are an artificial defense of centralization of power. This is not an attack on authority; but authority can be delegated, power cannot. Authority delegated is power lost.

Over the past five years, as a consultor to the Pontifical Commission for the Revision of the Code of Canon Law, I have become acquainted with many of the judges of the Roman tribunals. As one of my colleagues on the Commission

What Is the Problem?

aptly put it, "The more I work with these men [all priests, bishops or cardinals], the more I like and respect them, and the more I disagree with their ideas." The judges of the Roman tribunals are men of integrity and intelligence and frequently men of compassion. My experience with them leads me to believe that they are no more qualified, sometimes less qualified, than the judges in New York, Brooklyn, Buffalo, Pittsburgh, Hartford, Los Angeles or Chicago.

I am not judging their intelligence and knowledge of the law or their honesty and integrity; I am not referring to a degree of authority. I am saying that the judges of the Roman Rota rarely meet the parties to the cases or the witnesses whose testimony is essential to every decision (for in the law the testimony of the petitioning parties is always suspect). They are remote from the persons. Only one or two of them have any sense of the American idiom or way of speaking, which laces the testimony. Few appreciate the American expectation of due process with which we are so familiar.

A man has a right to be judged by his fellow man. Here is a further question. Should the persons who decide that a marriage is null and void or that a marriage which once existed may now be dissolved—should those who judge these matters be restricted to the clergy as distinct from the persons in the marriage under question? Are the clergy—be they pope, bishops, monsignors or parish priests—better equipped than lay persons—the parties themselves or their peers—to decide whether a marriage is null or dissoluble?

We, all of us, are the people of God. Christ founded the Church of the people of God. He did not set up the tribunals of the Catholic Church. Canon law with all its legal procedures and its tribunals and its system of adjudicating marriage cases is of human, ecclesiastical institution. It is well for us to bring to the attention of our religious leaders—the pope and the bishops—the anguish, the pain, the loss, the hate, the inhumanity, the lack of confidence and respect, the widespread injustice which is resulting from that human ecclesiastical institution. We must grope with them, our leaders, toward a more human and Christian way of bringing happiness and holiness into the lives of persons whose attempts to find fulfillment in marriage have failed and who now, more than ever, need help to settle their lives in a Christian home. They come seeking bread; will we give them stones?

II

Marriage and Divorce in Scripture

A number of texts of the Bible tell us what Jesus said about divorce and remarriage. Other texts give insights into the meaning of what he said. In two instances Jesus refers to passages in the Old Testament in order to explain his own teaching regarding marriage and divorce.

The two passages found in the Old Testament are the following: Genesis 1:27 which reads: "God created man in his image; in the divine image he created him; male and female he created them," and Genesis 2:22–24, which reads: "The man [Adam] said 'This one, at last, is bone of my bones and flesh of my flesh. This one shall be called "woman," for out of "her man" this one has been taken.' That is why a man leaves his father and mother and clings to his wife, and the two of them become one body." These two passages will be considered in the light of Jesus' statements about their application in the New Testament.

Of the four Gospel writers, John says nothing about Our Lord's statements on marriage. Matthew, Mark and Luke do. One phrase of Matthew poses something of a problem, but the passages from Mark and Luke appear to be clear, definite statements with little room for misunderstanding or interpretation.

Mark 10:2–12 reads: "Then some Pharisees came up and as a test began to ask him whether it was permissible for a husband to divorce his wife. In reply, he said, 'What command did Moses give you?' They answered, 'Moses permitted divorce and the writing of a decree of divorce.' But Jesus told them: 'He wrote that command for you because of your stubbornness. At the beginning of creation God made them male and female; for this reason a man shall leave his father and mother and the two shall become as one. They are no longer two but one flesh. Therefore, let no man separate what God has joined.' Back in the house again, the disciples began to question him about this. He told them 'Whoever divorces his wife and marries another commits adultery against her; and the woman who divorces her husband and marries another commits adultery.'"

Luke 16:18 reads: "Everyone who divorces his wife and marries another woman commits adultery. The man who marries a woman divorced from her husband likewise commits adultery."

Matthew 5:31, 32 reads: "It was also said, 'Whenever a man divorces his wife he must give her a decree of divorce.' What I say to you is: everyone who divorces his wife—lewd conduct is a separate case—forces her to commit adultery. The man who marries a divorced woman likewise commits adultery."

Matthew speaks again of divorce and remarriage in 19:3-12: "Some Pharisees came up to him to test him, 'May a man divorce his wife for any reason whatsoever?' He replied, 'Have you not read that at the beginning the Creator made them male and female and declared, "For this reason a man shall leave his father and mother and cling to his wife, and the two shall become as one?" Thus, they are no longer two but one flesh. Therefore, let no man separate what God has joined.' They said to him, 'Then why did Moses command divorce and the promulgation of a divorce decree?' 'Because of your stubbornness Moses let you divorce your wives,' he replied; 'but at the beginning it was not that way. I now say to you, whoever divorces his wife (lewd conduct is a separate case) and marries another commits adultery, and the man who marries a divorced woman commits adultery.' His disciples said to him, 'If that is the case between man and wife, it is better not to marry.' He said, 'Not everyone can accept this teaching, only those to whom it is given to do so. Some men are incapable of sexual activity from birth; some have been deliberately made so; and some there are who have freely renounced sex for the sake of God's reign. Let him accept this teaching who can.'"

"Lewd conduct is a separate case." This is the phrase used twice by Matthew, which poses a problem for Scripture scholars. There are those who say that in these words Our Lord recognizes the right of one whose conjugal rights have been violated by adultery to separate from the other party and to contract another marriage. Other scholars state that Our Lord was referring to marriages contracted between two Jews in violation of the Mosaic laws on consanguinity and affinity.

There are a number of reasons why I do not accept the first of these explanations of the words of Matthew and why I conclude that in the texts of the three Gospel writers, Jesus said clearly and distinctly, with no exceptive clauses, that marriage is indissoluble. Mark reports the words of Our Lord without qualification, and when the apostles question him a second time he substantially repeats his first statement again, without qualification. The brief statement of Luke is almost the same as the second statement of Jesus quoted by Mark. As we shall see in a few moments, Paul, who actually wrote his statement on divorce and remarriage before Mark and Luke, leaves room for no exceptive clauses in the words of Our Lord.

The great majority of Scripture scholars conclude that Mark, Luke and Matthew understood that Jesus was speaking of the indissolubility of all marriages—marriages between two Christians, marriages between a Christian and a non-Christian, marriage between two non-Christians. This is brought out very clearly in the Gospel of Mark where he quotes Jesus as saying that the indissolubility of marriage goes back to the beginning of creation. He proves his point by quoting the substance of the two aforementioned texts from the book of Genesis. Mark reports Jesus as saying that Moses permitted divorce only because of the stubbornness of the Jews. In the context of the other texts of Mark, Jesus' obvious reason for saying this is that he is countermanding the decree of Moses. *A New Catholic Commentary on Holy Scripture* comments in this way on verses twenty-three and twenty-four of the second chapter of Genesis: "Man and woman complement each other in the same human species; monogamous, indissoluble marriage was what God intended in the creation of man and woman." *The Jerome Biblical Commentary* notes that the unity of marriage and its monogamous nature are "God-willed."

Although some biblical scholars argue, with a degree of plausibility, that Matthew was introducing to the early Christian community a true exception to the general norm laid down by Jesus, I am not yet convinced of that claim. In the context of all of the statements in Chapter 19 of his Gospel, Matthew seems not to leave room for a true exception to the prohibition of Jesus against divorce. In much the same way as Mark, Matthew quotes Jesus as saying that the prohibition against divorce goes back to the creation of man and is inherent in the nature of man and woman as created by God. Matthew repeats the statement of Mark that Moses permitted divorce because of the hardness of heart of the Jews. In the account of Matthew it appears that the disciples clearly understood Jesus to exclude any exception to the prohibition against divorce since they said that if they accepted what Jesus said it would be preferable for them to remain single rather than to marry. In the time of Jesus, for a Jewish man to remain single voluntarily was almost inconceivable.

In Chapter 7 of Paul's First Letter to the Corinthians, verses 10 and 11, we read: "To those now married, however, I give this command (though it is not mine; it is the Lord's): a wife must not separate from her husband. If she does separate, she must either remain single or become reconciled to him again. Similarly, a husband must not divorce his wife." In the context of the letter, Paul is directing his words to Christians. However, since he speaks of this being the Lord's command and since the words echo the basic statements of Matthew, Mark and Luke, I conclude that Paul, too, understood the words to refer to all marriages, not only marriages between Christians. Those words are further proof that Jesus prohibited, without exception, divorce and remarriage.

In the verses immediately following, verses 12 to 14, Paul wrote as follows: "As for the other matters, although I know nothing the Lord has said, I say: If any brother has a wife who is an unbeliever but is willing to live with him, he must not divorce her. And if any woman has a husband who is an unbeliever but is willing to live with her, she must not divorce him. The unbelieving husband is consecrated by his believing wife; the unbelieving wife is consecrated by her believing husband. If it were otherwise, your children should be unclean; but as it is, they are holy."

In verses 15 and 16 Paul writes: "If the unbeliever wishes to separate, however, let him do so. The believing husband or wife is not bound in such cases. God has called you to live in peace. Wife, how do you know you will not save your husband, or you, husband, that you will not save your wife?"

It is most interesting to note that Paul, the first of the New Testament writers to state that Jesus unequivocally forbade divorce and remarriage, is the first of the followers of Jesus to say that there may be exceptions to this prohibition of Jesus. The legislation of the Catholic Church concerning this type of divorce, called the Pauline Privilege, is based upon the words of Paul.

In verses 15 and 16 Paul states that when two non-Christians are truly married, and one of them becomes a Christian, he is no longer bound by his marriage vows if he and his spouse are not able to live together in peace because of their irreconcilable religious differences. *The Jerome Biblical Commentary* interprets the words of Paul to mean that the newly converted Christian, by consenting to the departure of his non-Christian spouse, will be assuring for himself that peace which is the proper atmosphere of a Christian life. The *Commentary* goes on to say that the Christian is not obliged to oppose the separation and thus involve himself in a life of marital discord, mental antagonism and continued wrangling.

There are other observations to be made about the words of Paul and their application by the Church. Paul does not say that a divorce is permissible simply because one person is baptized and the other person is not baptized. On the contrary, he states that the couple should try to find happiness in their marriage even though this is the case. He clearly states that their irreconcilable approaches to life because of the difference in their religious beliefs, and their ensuing inability to live in peace, is the reason why divorce is permissible.

Moreover, he makes no mention of any intervention by the Church to certify that divorce under these conditions is permissible. I conclude that Paul was of a mind that the couple themselves were to make the decisions involved.

In an article in the *Journal of Ecumenical Studies* (6, 1969, pp. 53–63), Thomas L. Thompson strikes strongly at this point when he writes: "It should be noted that the whole traditional interpretation of the Pauline text as a special dispensation limited to marriages which are not sacramental is a misrepresentation of the grossest sort, not only because it treats the profound Pauline theology in a mechanical, legalistic manner, as something which can only be used in identical circumstances as a *privilege* to people who become Christian; but also it misreads the text which certainly does not allow the distinction between sacramental and non-sacramental marriages. In this passage Paul has clearly gone beyond the mere question whether divorce is to be allowed, and he points out the higher Christian value, such as 'the peace of the Lord,' and the fact that each man must live his life in consideration of these values."

It is my opinion that the exception mentioned by Paul refers only to marriages between Christians and non-Christians. Paul does not say, however, that only in such cases are divorces and remarriage lawful. As a matter of fact, his reason for making the exception is the inability of the couple to live in peace. His reason is not simply the fact that one party is a Christian and the other is not. With this reservation, I agree with the substance of Thompson's observations.

It is time that the Catholic Church faced up squarely to the fact that God in the Old Testament and Christ in the New Testament prohibited divorce in every marriage and not only in marriages in which both parties were baptized or in which there has been no physical intercourse. If she does not recognize the right to divorce and remarriage in intolerable marriages—marriages in which the couple cannot live together in peace—between persons who are baptized, she should not recognize the right to divorce and remarriage in any marriage. "Let no man separate what God has joined." Since the Church does not take these words literally or absolutely for marriages in which one or both parties are not baptized, she should not take them literally or absolutely for persons who are baptized. At our time in history it is clear from sociological, psychological and psychiatric studies that the simple fact that two persons have been baptized is no guarantee that their marriage will not become as intolerable as a marriage between two persons who have not been baptized.

Much the same thing can be said about the divorces that the Church grants simply because the married couple never had physical sexual intercourse. There is no provision for a divorce for this reason in the Bible. The Church certainly does not consider the marriage of Mary, the mother of Jesus, and St. Joseph, the foster father of Jesus, dissoluble because Joseph and Mary never had physical sexual intercourse. In all, or almost all, cases in which a divorce is granted because a couple did not have physical sexual intercourse the reason is that they were unable to adjust to each other in a psychological or emotional way. Their marriages never existed or died because they were unable to be persons with each other in a marital way, they were unable to be husband and wife with each other. They were unable to live in peace.

In her present use of the Pauline Privilege, the Petrine Privilege and in her granting of divorce because of the absence of physical intercourse, the Church *is actually already doing* what the Melchite Archbishop Elias Zogbi, an archbishop of the Roman Catholic Church, suggested during the Second Vatican Council: "It is a matter for the Church to decide on the opportuneness of admitting a new cause of dispensation analogous to those she has introduced in virtue of the Petrine Privilege." In a very gentle way, the Archbishop is saying that the Roman Catholic Church should do what the Orthodox Church has been doing since the time of Christ. The Orthodox Church has been upholding the doctrine of indissolubility as an ideal and a general imperative, but has not been cutting off from the Church couples who have reached a point where they can no longer seek the ideal or follow the imperative set down by Christ. For solid theological and sound moral reasons the Orthodox Christian Church has recognized and lived with a paradox. She has recognized the fact that some persons find it impossible to live up to the ideal established by God from the beginning of time and reasserted by Christ in the New Testament. She has found it repugnant to the infinite Compassion of Christ to conclude that a second marriage by these persons cuts them off from Christ or His Church.

Christ taught that marriage—*every* marriage whether it be a marriage between Christians or persons who are not Christians—is intended to be indissoluble. The words of Christ clearly state a general imperative that each couple strive for the ideal union of husband and wife. The Church must continue to teach and preach that indissolubility is intended to be a mark of *every* marriage. The Church cannot "grant" divorces. However, the Church can do as Paul did. She is already dissolving marriages for reasons other than those given by Paul. She can extend further her present practice of admitting the fact that dissolutions do occur; that couples who, to all intents and purposes, were truly married are no longer able to live together. She can recognize the fact that once a marriage is dead, there is no existential sign of a marital bond, natural or sacramental. She can admit the possibility of a new sign in a second marriage, with repentance when necessary, and with a renewed dedication to the ideal of indissolubility. The Church can do this so that persons may develop more completely as persons, and as Christians if they are Christian. It would be well for the Church to place more emphasis upon the words of Genesis 2:18: "The Lord God said: 'It is not good for man to be alone. I will make a suitable partner for him.'" If a man marries a woman who is not suitable to him, that is a tragedy. If he and his wife become irreconcilably unsuitable to each other, that is a tragedy. In either instance, the marriage is non-existent. In either instance it is still not good for man to be alone.

In the fifth chapter of the Gospel of Matthew, the very chapter in which he first quotes Christ concerning the indissolubility of marriage, Matthew sets down other imperatives of Our Lord. The Church has never considered these imperatives as absolute, as applicable in every case or as unexceptionable.

In verses 29 and 30, Matthew quotes Christ as saying: "If your right eye is your trouble, gouge it out and throw it away! If your right hand is your trouble, cut it off and throw it away!" It is obvious that Christ is telling us to use our eyes and our hands as instruments for good. It is clear that Christ is not telling us to mutilate ourselves. No one in his right mind could carry out these commands of Christ literally.

In verses 34 and 39 we find these words: "Do not swear at all. . . . Say 'Yes' when you mean 'Yes' and 'No' when you mean 'No.' Anything else is from the evil one." Despite this command of Christ, the Church, throughout her history, has made liberal use of oaths. They are used often in marriage tribunals.

In verses 39, 40 and 44 we read these words: ". . . offer no resistance to injury. When a person strikes you on the right cheek, turn and offer him the other. If anyone wants to go to law over your shirt, hand him your coat as well. . . . love your enemies." For good or evil, the Church has time and again made exceptions to these commands, has urged her members to make exceptions and has encouraged civil governments to do the same. She countenances self-defense and has often declared wars to be just.

Verse 48 contains the awesome command: ". . . you must be made perfect as your heavenly father is perfect." Obviously, Christ was telling us to strive for the ideal of being as perfect persons as possible. If the Church took this command literally, we would not have any persons fit to receive the Eucharist or any persons fit to celebrate the Eucharist.

In each of these four instances the Church has time and again admitted of abundant exceptions to the ideal or the general imperative explicitly stated by Christ. In our time in history it is incomprehensible that she does not see the need for further exceptions to the teaching concerning the indissolubility of marriage. In her present practice the Church has already gone far beyond the specific exception made by Paul. It is time the Church recognized this fact of life; that if any couple is irrevocably at war with one another psychologically and emotionally, they are incapable of possessing religious or spiritual peace.

In an article in the *Australian Catholic Record* (167, 1970, pp. 89–109), W. J. O'Shea offers these comments on the biblical evidence concerning divorce: "This ambiguity [of the biblical evidence] is confirmed: by the lack of unanimity on the question among the Fathers; by the wide variation found in the practice of the Christian Churches; and by the maze of interpretations proposed by biblical scholars. . . . The New Testament teaching is not so clear that it precludes the possibility of a change [in the teaching of the Church]."

As is clear from what I have already said, I do not consider the biblical evidence concerning divorce to be ambiguous. Yet, the Church has already made changes in her teaching as to when divorce and remarriage are possible within the law. Beginning with Paul, she has, at various times and in accordance with the needs of the times, made a number of morally acceptable exceptions to the ideal and imperative of Christ. In accordance with the needs of our times, the Church should further multiply these acceptable exceptions. This is the only way she can reconcile the principle of the indissolubility of marriage and the right of a person to live in a genuine integral marriage.

In an article in the *Irish Theological Quarterly* (37, 1970, pp. 199–209) Wilfrid Harrington writes: "Jesus prohibited divorce and that prohibition is absolute. But he prohibited divorce under the assumption that the marriage is a true marriage." I am reluctant to use the word "absolute" about Christ's teaching concerning divorce. The Church has too often disabled herself and her members by "absolutizing" ideas that were eventually proved to be wrong, or at least relative, conditional or subject to exceptions. I think we should consider Christ's unqualified prohibition of divorce to be an ideal that all married couples should try to attain, a moral imperative that would call upon all couples, before and after marriage, to make every possible effort to see to it that their marriages are indissoluble. When a couple are acceptable to each other in a first marriage we should presume, as they do, that their marriage is a true marriage. The same thing should be said about couples in second marriages. If a person enters a second marriage after the death of a first marriage, I think we should leave in God's hands the decision as to whether or not either or both marriages were true marriages.

In a lecture given at St. John's University in New York City on March 23, 1972, Myles M. Bourke, one of the foremost New Testament scholars in the United States, made the following statement: "Fidelity to the absolute prohibition of divorce made by Jesus does not mean that she [the Church] cannot make provision for the spiritual welfare [admission to the Eucharist] of those who have violated the prohibition of divorce, who have repented, but who are in new marriages which cannot be broken without grave spiritual and psychological harm to the parties involved."

On the basis of my reading of the works of other biblical scholars, I conclude that there is a consensus among these scholars as to the truth of the substance of Bourke's statement. As I have stated previously, I question the use of the word "absolute." I question, too, the emphasis upon the need for repentance. It is my experience that few marriages among persons trying to lead Christian lives break up because of willfully wrong words or actions. It is my experience, too, that there is a great deal of penance and suffering involved in the dying throes of marriages that ultimately become intolerable. Finally, as I will explain in detail when treating the "Good Conscience" solution, I do not think that admission to the Eucharist should be restricted to persons who have already entered second marriages. I think it should be extended to persons who, following the death of a first marriage, intend to enter a second marriage. It is my opinion that the Church should bless these second marriages when they take place.

I summarize my findings concerning the biblical evidence regarding divorce and remarriage as follows: (1) In the New Testament, Jesus Christ reaffirmed the Genesis teaching that, since man and woman were created, every marriage was intended by God to be indissoluble. Jesus does not indicate that there are to be any exceptions to this law. (2) I understand this teaching of Jesus to be an ideal that every married couple, aside from whether or not they are baptized, should try to attain. I understand this teaching to be a general imperative to every married couple without exception to strive for the ideal union of husband and wife. (3) Christ made no statement to the effect that a person who obtained a divorce and remarried would be permanently cut off from a union with God or with the Church. (4) Paul allowed exceptions to the teaching of Christ not because one party was baptized and the other was not baptized but because couples could not live in peace by reason of their irreconcilable religious differences.

III

Marriage and Divorce in Theology

When it is said that the teaching of the Church regarding marriage and divorce is based on Scripture, the statement can be understood only in the most rudimentary sense. That the Scriptures teach the ideal of the indissolubility of marriage is clear; but that the Scriptures also allow for exception, both in the Old Testament and in the New Testament, under specific circumstances is equally clear. The teachings of the Church, as we possess them today, are not immediately derived from Scripture; e.g., the absolute indissolubility of a valid, sacramental, consummated marriage; the relationship of baptism to matrimony as a sacrament; the dissolubility of a non-sacramental marriage; the dissolubility of a non-consummated marriage; the essence of matrimony being the marriage contract; the identity of the contract and the sacrament for baptized spouses; or the consummation of the sacramental union by carnal intercourse. Neither is the body of legislation regarding marriage derived immediately from Scripture; e.g., the list of diriment impediments; the conditions for validity; the causes for annulments; the procedures for dissolution; the penalties for not conforming to the law, etc.

In fact, it is accurate to say that the entire body of marriage legislation is based on theological presuppositions and is expressed in theological terms. To grasp the significance of the law regarding marriage and divorce, the theological base must be examined. Theological doctrine is itself the result of a dynamic of God's revelation being received into the processes of human life—being examined and interpreted by the human mind, being lived in the daily individual and communal life of the faithful and being developed through the historical processes of the Church in the world. The science

Marriage and Divorce in Theology

of theology is a secondary science; that is, it is necessarily derived from reflection on divine revelation as received in the human condition. Sources of theological reflection includes not only the sacred sciences, but all of human science and behavior. Manuals of theology enumerate Scripture, Apostolic tradition (the oral teachings to the earliest Christian communities); the Fathers of the Church (the first Christian leaders in Apostolic succession); the magisterium of the Church (the teaching of the popes and the councils); history (especially in evidence of universal consensus or dominant theological opinion); the practice of the faithful (where there is no clear teaching); philosophy; the natural and behavioral sciences; law and authority.

It would be impossible in many volumes to even attempt to assemble all the material from these many sources to support the thesis of this chapter that the present teaching of the Church on marriage and divorce is the result of a deformity in the normal theological development of doctrine. Fortunately, that doesn't have to be done because much study has already been completed by scholars in many of these areas of research, and a number of important articles and books on various aspects of the problem have recently been published. It should suffice for our purposes in this chapter to reflect on some of the major themes exposed by recent research.

*

Each day the scholarly evidence mounts that the Church has not always maintained the absolute indissolubility of marriage, although it has been a constant ideal set before the faithful as a goal to be devoutly desired and earnestly pursued. Christian love, peace, mercy and forgiveness are to keynote every marriage. Even in the case of adultery, the offended spouse was urged not to divorce, was taught that it was better to forgive and live in peace preserving the good of the family and society. In the constant practice of the East and frequent practice of the West, however, the Church showed herself tolerant of divorce and remarriage for grave reasons. While it considered the divorce a tragedy, the Church was willing to forgive the spouse guilty of causing the breakdown of the marriage if the person showed repentance for his or her sin.

To many Catholics today it seems a paradox that the Church could ever have taught one thing in theory and tolerate exactly the contrary in practice. The paradox is easily solved, however, if moral doctrine and pastoral practice are not confused with dogmatic doctrine and Church law. The teaching of the Church was not "law," it was the teaching of a moral ideal. To fail to attain the ideal in a given situation was not breaking the "law," it was a human failing to attain an ideal. The situation might call for repentance if the failure was caused by some sinful act, but the failure itself called for mercy and healing and a chance to try again. For centuries, the Church was not directly involved in the legal constitution of marriage or its dissolution.

In A.D. 331, for example, the Christian Emperor Constantine laid down the grounds for divorce which would prevail for all subjects, Christian or non-Christian. In a literal sense Roman law was being administered in the early Christian empire. Indeed, it was twenty years after the conversion of Constantine to Christianity. It is interesting that the grounds for divorce differed for husband and wife. The husband could be divorced if he were a murderer, a dealer in medicine or a destroyer of tombs, but not if he were a drunkard, a gambler or an adulterer. On the other hand, a wife could be divorced for adultery, if she used medicines for contraception or to induce abortion, or if she engaged in prostitution. She was not to be dismissed for minor faults or for any pretext.

Certain rather severe penalties were attached for anyone who broke the law and divorced a spouse without grounds. The penalty for the wife included loss of her property and deportation to an island for life. The penalty for the husband who put away his wife without sufficient grounds was loss of the wife's dowry and loss of the right to remarry. The approach to divorce and remarriage was substantially the same for several centuries.

Certain variations did occasionally appear under the direction of different emperors. In 499 Theodosius II expanded the list of valid grounds for divorce to include a number of immoral acts not directly connected with marriage; e.g., robbery, harboring a criminal, plotting against the empire, kidnapping. Adultery by either husband or wife became legal grounds for divorce.

By the time of Justinian's codification of the law (particularly Novel 22) in 535 the influence of Christian ideals could be detected in the development of marriage legislation. There was a growing awareness of the equality of men and women in laws concerning marriage and there was growing concern for the welfare of offspring. These developments did not affect the question of whether there could be divorce and remarriage. Rather, they provided that, in the event of divorce, the same grounds apply to men and women and that the offspring be properly cared for. Spouses were urged "not to sadden their procreated offspring by subsequent marriage," but should the parties remarry the law would regulate the distribution of property so that the children of the first marriage would not be deprived by a subsequent union. A waiting period before remarriage was imposed on the woman, not so much as a penalty or by reason of unequal treatment, but to avoid any confusion with regard to the rights of inheritance through the father.

By this time also, certain religious considerations had entered into the law and the legal processes, so it cannot be maintained that the laws on marriage were simply pagan laws which the Church opposed. In fact, bishops and even the pope were involved in the administration of the law.

The law itself contained a religious justification for dissolution of marriage; i.e., entering a convent or monastery under religious vows by either party amounted to consensual divorce and the other had the right to remarry. The bishops were involved in the divorce processes in other ways; e.g., by presiding in civil courts and later in the "Episcopal Court." When the penalty for a wife attempting divorce without sufficient grounds was changed from "exile" to an island to confinement in a monastery, the Church was responsible for administering the sentence. In this way the Church was instrumental in the dissolution of the marriage, for the husband was then free to remarry.

After meticulous examination of the legal practices of this period, John T. Noonan, Jr., concluded, "The calm acceptance of dissolubility by the law shows that at this time, between 331 and 566, no definitive Christian position had been established on remarriage and divorce." (*Bond of Marriage*, ed., William Bassett, p. 87.) Victor Pospishil finds that although there are explicit prohibitions of remarriage in the writings of some of the Fathers of the Church, they are usually conditioned in that they refer to divorces for reasons other than adultery, or they refer only to one party to the divorce; e.g., the prohibition of the wife to remarry. He concludes that, "The right of the husband to divorce an adulteress wife was always upheld, and he was considered justified in marrying another woman (Origen, Lactantius, Basil the Great, Ambrosiaster, Asterius of Amasea, Epiphanius of Salamis, Victor of Antioch, Avitus of Vienna; [the Councils of] Arles (314), Milvis (416), Vannes (461), Agde (506)." A little later he adds, "Some Fathers felt obliged to permit innocent wives, maliciously deserted by their husbands, to remarry. These and other relaxations were granted by the Fathers in the belief that such mercy or condescension (Origen, Basil the Great) behooved the Church." (*Divorce and Remarriage*, Herder and Herder, N.Y., 1967, pp. 51 and 52.)

For another five centuries the laws regulating the grounds for divorce fluctuated between laxity and severity in various places and at various times. With Theodore of Canterbury, Venerable Bede, Boniface of Mainz, Egbert of York and others, voluntary and involuntary desertion was grounds for divorce. Local synods and the penitential books (books written to assist priests in administering the Sacrament of Penance to the faithful in a uniform manner, at least within a certain diocese or district) give evidence that the practice of divorce and remarriage had widespread acceptance, and in certain instances divorce was almost completely unlimited. Mutual consent to divorce was the only requirement needed in the Formularies of Angers (sixth century) and of Marculf (seventh century).

Certain reforms counterbalanced the laxity and abuse of almost unlimited divorce. The Carolingian reform, the Cluny reform and the Gregorian reform all sought to re-establish Christian ideals of the highest order, and this included the teaching and practice regarding the indissolubility of marriage. There was not, however, any evidence of genuine dogmatic or sacramental development of doctrine regarding marriage.

For the first thousand years of the two thousand years of Christian history both in the East and the West the indissolubility of marriage was taught as an ideal of matrimony both for the faithful and for infidels. With varying degrees of legal restrictions, however, divorce and remarriage were always permitted without condemnation in the East, and the practice was at least tolerated at various times and places in the West. The traditional handling of divorce and remarriage continues in the East even to today. But the teaching on marriage was to take another direction in Rome and the Christian West.

Movements and influences which often take centuries to develop sometimes converge at a particular period in history and, as light rays passing through a lens, project a new or different image into the future. The first two centuries of the second millennium of Christianity was just such a decisive period in the development of the teaching of the Roman Church about and its legislation on marriage.

The feudal system placed great emphasis on property rights and blood relationship arising from marriage, and to insure family continuity and rights, strict regulation was needed to control marriage and its civil effects. In this matter, monarchs found in the bishops of the Church stalwart allies. Placed in positions of power with both civil and religious jurisdiction, bishops could control the turmoil of a rising aristocracy and territorial conflicts of lords and vassals. The hierarchy was particularly suited to the purpose of monarchs and princes because the rule of celibacy by which the episcopacy lived prevented them from beginning a succession of hereditary power. The Church became the custodian of the civil legislation as well as the sacramental administration of marriage. Bishops in the West were with ever greater frequency being called on to solve marriage cases and at the same time the more difficult decisions were sent to the Roman Pontiff, whose influence and power in both the civil and religious spheres were on the ascendancy. Over a long periods the teaching on the formation and indissolubility of marriage progressed by way of a few rudimentary canons to a large collection of decisions, solutions, decrees, advisories and opinions which were vastly unequal in authority and influence and almost totally lacking in coherence and consistency. The reasons given for most solutions were based on the authority of other decisions of the Fathers and of papal decrees, rather than on reasons intrinsic to the nature of marriage or the specifics of the case.

The critical time of the first attempts at a consistent and systematic codification of the law coincided with the first attempts to introduce a systematic presentation of the teachings of the Church. The "Decree of Gratian" (1140) marked the beginning of the Science of Canon Law in the application of scholastic methodology to the study of the Roman decrees and the accumulation of ecclesiastical decisions and directives. The *Sentences of Peter Lombard* was one of the most influential *summas* of the early scholastic period. One of St. Thomas Aquinas' major works is his commentary of the *Sentences of Peter Lombard*. Aquinas' own masterpiece *Summa Theologica* was never completed so that the section of the *Summa* on marriage is taken from his commentary on the *Sentences*.

The years immediately following the appearance of Gratian's and Lombard's works were marked by continuing disputes on the question of the formation of the matrimonial bond. This was also the period of the rise of the scholastic universities, and two of the greatest of these were at odds on the subject. The Bologna school insisted on the necessity of carnal relations to form the matrimonial bond. Those of the Paris school held that marriage was true and complete by reason of mutual consent to the marriage contract. Peter Lombard and Peter of Potiers were of the latter opinion. Adhering to one or the other position had serious social consequences at that time. It was relatively common practice for parents of the aristocracy to arrange for the marriage of their children in order to promote peace between families or in order to settle property claims or make political or military alliances. Since the ceremonial and material arrangements were often made months or years before the couple had the opportunity to cohabit, it happened that sometimes one or the other would in the interim attempt another marriage and actually consummate it. If the second marriage was challenged by a party of the first wedding, the question was "Which was the valid marriage?" Those who believed in the opinion of the Bologna school would say the second was the only valid marriage; those in Paris would claim the first was valid for consent without copulation was sufficient to form the indissoluble bond.

The difficulties arising from the diverse opinions regarding what constituted the valid marriage—consent or consummation—had far-reaching social implications, and it was critical that the problem be resolved. The resolution came by way of papal responses. In the West, papal authority had reached a dominance so decisive that the responses from Rome were not only respected as moral directives, but accepted as expressions of law for all the Christian Churches.

※

The papal responses to resolve these and other marriage problems during this critical period influenced the direction the theology of marriage would take in the West for centuries to come. Alexander III (1159–81) had been a student of Gratian and a professor of canon law at Bologna before becoming pope. In his early works he held Gratian's position that both consent and carnal consummation were essential in forming the marital bond. In accordance with this opinion he listed several causes for the dissolution of non-consummated marriages. He proposed, with certain misgivings, that a second marriage which was consummated took precedence over a first marriage which was not consummated. He later modified this position. As pope, he issued hundreds of decrees which, in spite of some rather ambiguous decisions, held that "present consent" was binding even without copulation. In a response to the Archbishop of Salerno he added other conditions to make the marriage binding. If a girl gave present consent to her spouse, in the presence of witnesses, according to the custom of the locality, she could not marry another. If she did attempt another marriage and even completed the union with carnal relations, she must be returned to the previous spouse. This is apparently a reversal of his earlier position, but he said, this decision is to stand "even though others may have different opinions and despite the fact that our predecessors may have judged otherwise."

During his pontificate and in subsequent years the position became more widely accepted that marriage was essentially constituted by consent and that consummation added perfection to the union by making it a complete sign of the union of Christ with his Church and by giving it perfect stability—i.e., rendering it absolutely indissoluble. It should be noted here that the practical decisions of the popes were becoming not only normative of action, but gradually they were becoming normative and restrictive of theological reflection.

Alexander III, in the course of handing down decisions, had included the following scriptural interpretations:

> The scriptural text "Everyone who puts away his wife, save on account of immorality, causes her to commit adultery," teaches the indissolubility of marriage only in reference to matrimony consummated by "carnal copula."
>
> The scriptural text "A man shall leave his father and mother, and shall cleave to his wife; and they shall be two in one flesh" refers simply to carnal intercourse.

and the following theological opinions:

> Man and woman are not "one flesh" until they have consummated their union with carnal copulation.
>
> Carnal intercourse is the only way that marriage can be consummated.

These interpretations of scripture and theological opinions were cited in support of administrative decisions without further theological justification or elaboration. Actually, the decisions were never intended to be treatises on scriptural or theological doctrine, but resolutions of practical problems. The compilations and codification of decisions prevalent during this period often omitted the specific details pertinent to the cases being resolved. Emphasis, however, was placed on the "doctrinal" content. An example of the editorial work on the law is evidenced in the collection of St. Raymond of Pennafort when he added a theological qualification to the words of a decree of Alexander III to make the "doctrine" consistent, and when he omitted decrees or parts of decrees which were opposed to the doctrinal or "teaching" objectives of his work. (Cf. *The Indissolubility Added to Christian Marriage by Consummation*, James Coriden, Catholic Book Agency, Rome, 1961, pp. 12, 16.) To strive for consistency in the law is a necessity; to provide a consistent code for the teaching of the law is laudible; but for theological reflection, for theological development of doctrine, the distortion or elimination of opposed opinions is absurd. That is why the provisions of law may be one of the valid sources of theological reflection, but they can never be the sole source. Law is ordered to a single mode of action, not to the presenting and weighing of doctrinal opinions that might be quite opposed or contrary if not contradictory. The reasons adduced to support a decision or to justify a law do not necessarily have any doctrinal value.

This is quite apparent in a decision of Alexander III. He supported his position on the effect of consummation on the indissolubility of marriage by appealing to a fanciful legend commonly believed in medieval times. According to the story, the marriage feast of Cana was the wedding banquet of St. John the Evangelist, and it was at these very nuptials and before St. John's marriage could be consummated that Our Lord called St. John to be his beloved disciple. Alexander accepted this legend and used it to support the papal power of dissolving a marriage for the sake of religious life and for showing the added stability and absolute indissolubility of a consummated marriage. Although the legend has no doctrinal value, the use of it in a papal decree gave credibility and longevity to the belief far beyond its intrinsic worth. In much the same way, scriptural and theological opinions and interpretations in the decisions of the popes assumed an unwarranted doctrinal power that was to have a profound effect on theological development.

If this phenomenon was evident in Pope Alexander III and in the pontificates of Lucius III, Urban III, Gregory VIII, Clement III and Celestine III, it reached its zenith in the extraordinary pontificate of Innocent III, who reigned from 1198 to 1216. Innocent III, the nephew of Celement III, had trained in theology, civil and canon law in the schools of

Rome, Paris and Bologna. When only thirty-seven years of age he became pope. He brought great energy to the papacy and great learning and determination to the cause of reforming all of Christendom.

He undertook significant negotiations with the civil powers of Europe and established crusades against the Albigensians and Saracens, and he made every effort to unite Christian princes and reform society. He convened the Fourth Lateran Council in 1215 for the reform of the universal Church and established the great mendicant orders, such as the Dominicans and Franciscans, and brought reform to religious and monastic life. In regard to marriage doctrine and practice, Innocent closely followed the school of thought established by Alexander III and his successors. At Bologna, Innocent had been the student of Hugh of Pisa the greatest canon law expert at the time. The *Summa* of Hugh of Pisa, written about 1188, was the most extensive and authoritative commentary on law during this period. The widespread influence of this book, together with the fact that in theory and in practice it was adopted by the powerful Pope Innocent III, firmly established the position of Alexander III throughout the Christian West.

Early in the pontificate of Innocent III it seemed that he might become even more severe than his predecessors in his judgment regarding the indissolubility of marriage. He permitted the dissolution of the non-consummated marriage for only one reason other than death, and that was entrance into religious life. He admitted this one exception only with great reluctance and only because he hesitated to change the practice of his predecessor. (Coriden, Ibid., p. 48.)

During the period from the beginning of the reign of Alexander III through the reign of Innocent III the law had established that the essence of marriage consisted in the consent to the contract, and its perfection as a contract and as a sacrament consisted in consummation by carnal intercourse. The only exception to the law of absolute indissolubility was the dissolution of a non-consummated marriage for the sake of religious life. These tenets of law were derived from papal decrees concerned with the discipline of the faithful within a given society and in answer to specific problems and ques-

Marriage and Divorce in Theology

tions relevant to the times. These specific decrees in compilations or in the hands of the pope became universal law and the law became, by an incredible inversion of theological development, the doctrine on marriage and divorce. The theological development of marriage doctrine had been effectively strapped into the strait jacket of law, and it has yet to be released.

What had happened becomes dramatically clear if we go back in thought to the time of the separation of East and West in 1054. At that time the theory and the practice of the East and West were, at least, tolerably the same regarding marriage and divorce. Both East and West taught the indissolubility of marriage at least as the ideal of Christian matrimonial life. Yet in the face of reality, where Christian ideals are not always attained, with sorrow and enough reluctance to keep the practice restricted to grave cause, the Church consistently allowed divorce and remarriage in the East and, for over a thousand years, at least tolerated the practice at certain times and places in the West. Then in the course of two hundred years, while the Eastern theory and practice remained constant, the Church of Rome took a determined stand in opposition to divorce and remarriage. Notably in the fifty-seven years from Alexander III to Innocent III the more strict discipline was established and solidified.

In the West of 1250 indissolubility was no longer a Christian ideal for which every couple should strive; it was a "law" which everyone had to accept. And it was more than a law; it was accepted by most scholastics as a doctrinal teaching of dogmatic character located in sacramental theology. This was the period of the great scholastic syntheses of doctrine, and reflection on marriage was confined to the elaboration of the legal theory of consent, contract and consummation. Because it was so confined it lost the rich tradition of marriage being a living union of a couple who together enter into a new Kingdom with Christ striving through mutual love, affection and fruitfulness to perfect that union until it shows forth the sign of the undivided unity of Christ with his Church.

The truncation of the theology of marriage led Karl Barth to comment that the Roman Catholic Church has a theology of the wedding ceremony and the first night, but it does not have a theology of matrimony.

I believe that the root problem in the Catholic approach to marriage, both theological and legal, goes back to the time when the "nature and ideals" of marriage became the subject of papal "legislation," and this was, in turn, converted into dogmatic teachings of the Church. Once that conversion was made, once the ideal of indissolubility became an absolute of the legal bond and a dogmatic tenet of the ordinary magisterium, the whole of the theology of marriage was dislocated and the possibility of genuine doctrinal development eliminated. Champions of absolute indissolubility proclaimed the purity of their doctrine, and as one scholar has remarked there was ample evidence that the position hardened into doctrine because it displayed the doctrinal superiority of the Church of Rome as protector of the sacraments and defender of the faith. Just how much there was of pride or display or any other extrinsic motivation is most difficult to determine, and whatever the conjectures of scholars who have dwelled on this period, one fact is clear, the theology of marriage was smothered in the confusion of discipline and doctrine. The confusion persisted, and some churchmen made every effort to have the position regarding indissolubility solemnly defined as official doctrine of the Church. It never happened.

Pope Eugene IV's *Decretum pro Armenis*, which was included in the Acts of the Council of Florence in 1438, states, "Although it is permitted to separate matrimonial cohabitation because of fornication, it is nevertheless not allowed to contract another marriage, because the bond of marriage which was lawfully contracted is perpetual." Many theologians including such prominent and influential scholars as Vasquez, Suarez and Billot considered the statement to be a dogmatic definition of the absolute indissolubility of marriage. Less triumphant scholarship, however, reveals that the decree is not issued as an infallible decision nor is it a true conciliar document. The same pope at the same Council of Florence heard the representatives of the Eastern Churches defend their practice of allowing divorce and remarriage on the grounds that the practice was in conformity with the Gospel and the teachings of the Fathers of the Church. Although Pope Eugene did not agree with them in theory or in practice, neither did he find their position a doctrinal obstacle to reunion of the East and West. Pospishil concludes that the decree "is nothing else than an authoritative instruction governing pastoral practice." (*Divorce and Remarriage*, p. 62.)

Another very serious attempt to define the doctrine of indissolubility came in the Council of Trent. The Protestant Reformation had challenged the Roman Catholic Church's teaching and practice regarding marriage and divorce. The Council of Trent was the response of the Church to the Reformation. This apparently was the historical time and place to define once and for all the doctrine of the indissolubility of marriage if it was ever to be defined as a doctrine of the Church. Many of the Fathers of the Council considered it such, and the first draft proposal on the subject was a clear condemnation of divorce and remarriage even as practiced in the Eastern Churches. Many other Fathers at the Council, however, objected to the formulation, and a lengthy debate ensued. The canon was divided and substantially changed. The final formulation of Canon 7, which was chosen by the majority of the Fathers of the Council of Trent, was approved by the pope and promulgated as the official teaching of the Church, does not condemn the theory or the practice of the Eastern Churches regarding divorce and remarriage. In fact, it is carefully worded to avoid any such implication by turning the focus of the canon away from the question of indissolubility of marriage and directing it to the inerrancy of the Roman Church when she taught or teaches that the bond of marriage cannot be dissolved because of adultery of either spouse. There is no doubt that the Roman Church taught the indissolubility of marriage; there is no doubt that she teaches it today. There is serious doubt, however, whether she teaches the indissolubility of marriage as a discipline to be followed in practice or as a doctrine to be believed. And there is even graver doubt that the Church intends or ever intended to define dogmatically the absolute indissolubility of marriage as an integral part of divine revelation.

Without reciting the long list of theological opinions on this point, it is sufficient to point out that following the Council of Trent the Church did not limit or restrict its power to dissolve marriage. In fact, it expanded that power considerably by freely applying the Pauline Privilege and the papal dissolution of the non-consummated marriage. Beginning with the missionary activity after the discovery of the New World, during the colonization of pagan lands, though to the acceptance of the modern pluralistic society as a fact of life, the Church has constantly expanded the use of the Petrine Privilege; i.e., the dissolution of a marriage (in which at least one spouse is unbaptized) in favor of the Faith.

The justification for these practices of the Church cannot be based on direct recourse to Divine Revelation. The present teaching of the Church on the nature of marriage, the present legislation governing its canonical effects, and the present practice of the popes, the Curia, and the tribunals are simply not contained in Divine Revelation, and I do not believe they are even based on good theology.

Scripture clearly states the marriage ideal and it clearly proclaims the sacredness of the matrimonial union—"Let no man separate what God has joined." Matthew, Mark and Luke express Christ's teaching on indissolubility, while Paul, and possibly Matthew, cite exceptions in the New Covenant even as there had been exceptions in the Old Covenant. St. Paul gave the sacramental symbolization of matrimony when he said that the union of man and wife in one flesh is likened to the great mystery of the union of Christ with his Church. Yet none of these sources reveals when a couple were joined by God; when a true marriage had taken place; what constitutes the marriage bond; what conditions have to be met for its valid reception; what conditions render the attempt to marry null and void; who is physically, mentally, emotionally capable of entering the marital union; what ratifies a marriage; what effect intercourse has on the marriage; what constitutes an act apt to generate; what the meaning of consummation is and what effect it has on the union; precisely in what the sacrament of matrimony consists; what is the meaning of the exceptions to indissolubility; whether there are, in fact, other exceptions not literally cited in Scripture. Not one of these questions is settled by Scripture.

All of these questions and many more were asked during

the course of centuries and they were answered in a variety of ways by any number of the Fathers of the Church, by bishops and patriarchs and synods and councils and popes. And the fact remains that none of these questions has ever been answered in a way that pertains to the dogmatic definition of the Church.

It is my contention that our present answers to these questions from the principal one—What is the nature of marriage?—to the one that has caused the most controversy and the most human suffering—What is the indissolubility of the bond?—are the result of basic confusion at different levels, between the ideal and the real, between legal discipline and theological doctrine, between moral teaching and dogmatic definition.

Further, it is my contention that this confusion was the result of building a structure of marriage doctrine on the limited, legalistic concepts and interpretations of contract, consent, bond, sacrament, consummation, indissolubility. In the law these concepts received an entity, a being, a reality, completely apart from the reality of the marriage of two human beings. And when the law regarding the contract and its effects was taken as the teaching of the Church on the nature of marriage, theology, rather than reflecting on the reality of marriage, reflected on these woefully inadequate concepts. That fact was brought home to me by the story of a professor in a pontifical seminary which took great pride in teaching theology directly from such sources as the *Summa Theologica of St. Thomas Aquinas*. When the professor came to the tract on matrimony he told the students not to bother reading St. Thomas on marriage "because the canons on which St. Thomas based his theology were superseded by the Code of Canon Law promulgated in 1918." It is true, the so-called "theology" of marriage has been based on canon law since the thirteenth century. Marriage is the one area of theology in which the law has led the reflection, the law has limited the reflection so that it can truly be said that the Church does not really have a theology of marriage and divorce—all it has is the law. And that law is now a historical anachronism. It is irrelevant and needs to be changed— radically.

IV

The Meaning of Marriage

The Catholic Church is in desperate need of a theology of marriage that will reflect the reality of the personal, social and sacramental dimensions of matrimony in the world today. Only such a theology will be adequate to serve realistically the Christian community and to assist pastorally the individuals who are preparing for marriage; the couples who are married and raising families; the families who are experiencing marriage problems; the spouses who are suffering intolerable marriages; the divorced couples who are seeking to remarry; and the remarried couples who are seeking the sacraments. These are the human needs that cry out for attention; these are the questions that call for meaningful answers; these are the conditions that beg for understanding and mercy; and these are the realities with which present marriage instruction, marriage law and marriage tribunals of the Church cannot cope.

It would be presumptuous to suggest that such a theology could even be outlined here, although I think it is important at least to consider that the dimensions of a realistic theology of marriage would extend far beyond the definitions of our present teaching and far beyond the delineations of our present law. The search today should not be for better definitions and greater justice in the law; rather the search should be for greater meaning in the reality we all witness or in some measure experience; for greater significance in our efforts to realize Christian ideals; and for greater mercy when, in human weakness, we fail to attain those ideals.

*

It is difficult—perhaps impossible—to define any living being. There is even a profound inadequacy in the general description of marriage as the union of two persons, a man and a woman, who so come together that they personally complement one another as utterly as is humanly possible, to the good of themselves, each other, their children as well as the local, religious and world communities. This full union of persons carries with it the dynamics of mutual growth and fruitfulness, unquestioning faithfulness and taken-for-granted lastingness which cannot be contained in words and takes a lifetime to live. The physical, emotional, mental and spiritual make-up of men and women is such that children are ordinarily the result of marriage. The greater the vitality, the fuller the complementation of a man and a woman in all areas, the more likely it is that they will be good parents. The children who result from particular marriages are dependent on many circumstances. Among the considerations that should determine the size of the family are, for example, the ability of a couple to be fit parents to one or more children; their age; their economic situation; their emotional, mental and physical health, as well as their religious outlook on life.

The present Jewish, Catholic and Protestant ideals of marriage are not substantially different as is witnessed in their marriage ceremonial rituals. It may well be that, not only in official religious teaching, but in the minds, and particularly in the emotions and hearts of Jews, Catholics and Protestants the initial total commitment in marriage is an effort to assuage the restlessness of which Augustine spoke when he said, "Our hearts are restless, Lord, and they shall not rest until they rest in Thee."

Whatever may be said about the purpose of marriage being the preservation of the species, about the objectives of marriage as a social or religious responsibility; for the spouses, marriage is first of all formed and experienced in its personal dimension.

※

MUTUAL FRUITFULNESS, FAITHFULNESS, LASTINGNESS—these three dynamics are the vital elements in every marriage. Mutual fruitfulness, faithfulness and lastingness are to be liberating and freeing dynamics so that a couple in marriage not only complement each other but they complete themselves.

The truth is nowhere more evident than in marriage, any reservation in any of these three areas is a disorder that may breed discontent, selfishness, suspicion and perhaps the tragedy of a broken marriage.

FRUITFULNESS is the key element in marriage. It involves the complementation, the completing—the continual complementation and completing—of the man and the woman as persons. By and through and in marriage each should grow, each should become a more full, a more complete person. The marriage should draw out the dignity and the goodness of each. The paradox is that each completes herself and himself by completing the other person. The complementation of the union of partners breeds the completeness of each partner. While we ordinarily think of children as the fruit of marriage, the "first fruit" of marriage is the growth of the partners as persons. This growth derives from the giving, often self-sacrificing giving, of the partners to each other.

FAITHFULNESS of the partners in marriage is a prerequisite for continued and growing fruitfulness. Faithfulness is the concerned awareness of the partners for each other, the utter and unreserved, almost abandoned, giving of the partners one to another—physically, emotionally, mentally, spiritually—so that the thought of any form of marital affection for or with another person is alien to their giving of themselves to each other. The need and desire for fruitfulness and growth breeds faithfulness and the two together breed lastingness. A self-giving, faithful fruitfulness can never tolerate the sharing of marital affection with another or others.

LASTINGNESS results from the continual personal need for an ever deeper probing of the mystery of the completing of a man and a woman in their mutual giving and growing. The fulfillment of each is found in the intimate faithfulness with its vision that even death will not part them with finality. Ideally, marriage may lead to as ultimate a complementation and completion as a man and a woman may find on earth.

Many of us grew up with the false idea that a man is always the head of a family and a woman is always the heart. This is just not so. Each marriage is unique and possibly not even a particular couple are aware of how much of the head

The Meaning of Marriage

and how much of the heart each partner gives to the marriage. Marriage is a mutual giving of heart and head, body and mind, a mutual complementation of perfections and imperfections. Marriage is a dignified unselfish giving of a man to a woman and a woman to a man.

Marriage then is first of all a personal union of two human beings each of whom is unique. Each has a life uniquely his own. Each is a mature person who has chosen life—only that and at whatever risk—who never lets life leak out or lets it wear away by the mere passage of time. When a person withholds giving and spending life, he or she chooses nothing.

In marriage each of two mature persons choose each other in life. The union is the mutual will to live in oneness—the oneness of love, the oneness of sharing life and its fortunes and its future together. When persons in marriage do not give and spend their lives in and with and for each other, their marriage is dying. Each marriage to continue to be genuine must be uniquely alive. The fluidity and dynamism of the individual living person is magnified in marriage.

Because every marriage is a union of two unique persons, each marriage has a special uniqueness beyond description. The personal love of a man and woman for each other make it so. Their mutual love says loud and clear:

- A will to oneness.
- A will to mutual fruitfulness.
- A will to mutual faithfulness.
- A will to lifelong lastingness.

Genuine, true and complete marriage is effected in the free, loving will of a man and a woman to live as one—the union is effectively forged of a will-to-oneness in life. The bond is constantly maintained in a continued will-to-oneness. This personal dimension of marriage is true marriage. It possesses and displays the essential elements of the marital union effected by mutual love—a will-to-oneness which has an intrinsic order to personal and mutual fruitfulness, faithfulness and lastingness.

I believe that the teaching and the law of the Church has overemphasized the preservation of the species as the primary consideration of marriage. The law dwells needlessly on the procreation of children, on physical potency to perform acts apt to generate offspring and on the performance of carnal intercourse for the consummation of the union. It is ludicrous that an old couple who wish to enter a union of mutual affection and share their twilight years together can be justified before the law only if each intends "to give the right to perform acts which are apt to generate," even though they are not apt to perform such acts, and if they did, the acts would not be apt to generate. Although St. Thomas Aquinas' tract on marriage in the supplement of the *Summa* is nothing more than the rationalization of the prevailing law in the form of a commentary on the *Sentences* of Peter Lombard, he did not in his more mature theological reflection fall into the trap of legalism when discussing the marriage of St. Joseph and the Blessed Virgin. The first and formal perfection of marriage he claims consists in an "inseparable union of souls, by which husband and wife are pledged by a bond of mutual affection that cannot be sundered." (*Summa* III, Q 29, a. 2.)

*

It is true, of course, that the basic instincts both for sexual union and for procreation are best brought to climax and fruition in that loving and stable union of love between one man and one woman. Preservation of the species is the normal and natural and desirable result of loving union of a man and a woman. Monogamous union is naturally ordered to the personal and mutual satisfaction of lovers, to the generation and continued welfare of the offspring and to the good order of society. Procreation does not make a man and woman any more husband and wife than before, but it does add the new dimension of parenthood and creates the basic unit of society —the family.

A theology of marriage today must be aware of and reflect on the total society of which the family is a part. The teaching and laws that guided and governed a feudal society, a predominantly rural society, a provincial, ethnic, nationalistic society must of necessity be different in a modern world society. Modern society and modern culture display different behavioral patterns from those of the past. The value and dignity of each individual person, including the child and youth, as well as the unqualified equality of men and women as persons must be recognized and respected. What was once a protective family circle of parents and children, grandparents and uncles and aunts and cousins living in close proximity and often living off the same land has all but ceased in America and with its passing the traditional family ties have diminished.

The mobility of population, the right of a woman to pursue a career other than housewife, the less and less likelihood that a man and woman will be tied to a particular place, a particular job or job location—all these are facts of life of a changing social culture. These very facts and values call for marriage to reach out in its social dimension and enrich it through personal and social fruitfulness, faithfulness and lastingness. In its social dimension marriage shows forth its fruitfulness in children, its faithfulness in the unity of the nuclear family and its lastingness in the stability of family ties whatever the divisions of time or space. There is more and more value to a man and a woman today being more broadly and deeply entwined with one another as persons and with their children as persons if they are to avoid rootlessness and wandering.

The "good old days" were good when they were young and vigorous days. The riches and the joys of the good old days will be—and can be—found in the new and good and visionary days in which we live.

※

That matrimony is a sacrament has been a traditional teaching of the Church. What the sacramentality of marriage really means has, since the thirteenth century, been traditionally neglected by the Church. Although the Church of Rome has given much attention to the subject of marriage, it has been preoccupied with defending the sacredness of marriage, of protecting the sacrament from personal abuse and from the incursion of secular powers over its sacred trust. I do not mean that this preoccupation has not had some historical justification. The fact remains, however, that today we lack a theology of marriage not only in its personal and social dimensions but, even more tragically for the Church, in its sacramental dimension.

The triumph of the Roman Church in the battle for indissolubility and the outlawing of divorce under the banner of protecting the sacramental bond brought with it an incalculable loss of the sense of the sacramentality of marriage. To gird for the battle, the Catholic Church in the West had to overemphasize intensely the contractual aspect of marriage and the legal bond that resulted from consent to the contract. The very idea of "contract" is limited. Of its nature a contract is a cold, legal instrument which, in most instances, is conceived and executed with healthy, self-interested calculation. Thus, even when parties to a contract are friends, the contract necessarily sets up limitations, reservations, safeguards, guarantees of fulfillment, conditions of continuation and termination.

It is undoubtedly true that marriage has social effects that must be controlled contractually to preserve equity for the parties and to maintain order in society. However, to confine and restrict the nature and essence of marriage to contractual terms ignores the reality that in marriage two wills are formed in oneness of life and being. The avowal of mutual love in fruitfulness, faithfulness and lastingness, which most couples truly intend when they marry, cannot be contained in contract. Matrimony is not the consent itself, but the union of persons directed to one purpose—a common life. Matrimony is not the contract as some third thing apart from the common life initiated through mutual consent. The bond of marriage is not something distinct from the dynamic of the personal, social and sacramental relationship of mutual fruitfulness, faithfulness and lastingness lived through mutual consent.

In order to control the legal effects of a couple joining in matrimony, in order to determine the social effects of the marital union, the law had to "freeze" certain moments in the dynamic of life and identify them as signifying that indeed certain events in the personal, social and sacramental order were taking place and could be publicly witnessed or verified. Consent before a priest and two witnesses became the instrument of entering into matrimony. Matrimony became the contract. The indissoluble bond became the effect. Within these static constructs marriage relationship could now be legally contained and its effects conveniently controlled.

To these "frozen" moments theologians attached the sacramental signification. Suarez and Bellarmine, for example, identified "sacrament" and "contract" in matrimony. They were for these theologians the same and inseparable reality. Among Christians, wherever there was marital "contract" there was "sacrament." Others distinguished the intention of marriage from the intention of receiving the sacrament. They were not the same. It was possible to intend marriage and not to intend to receive the sacrament. Therefore, the contract and the sacrament were not the same thing in reality. Although there were various nuances, for most theologians the sign was basically the same. The union of man and wife was a sacramental sign of the union of Christ with his Church.

Unfortunately, because "sacramentality" was attached to the "contractual" concept derived from the law, the sacrament was "frozen" also. Matrimony became a sacrament that was administered and received by a couple in the act of exchanging consent to a contract. Matrimony was an "event" sacrament, like baptism. Baptism was performed by pouring water over the head of the one to be baptized and pronouncing the words. Matter and form were brought together in the liturgical ceremony and, "bingo," it was done once and for all. Marriage was conceived in much the same way. Two baptized persons exchange marital vows according to the form of the Church, and it was done for good and forever.

Baptism is indeed an "event" sacrament, just as is the Sacrament of Penance and the celebration of the Eucharist. Baptism is an initiation, a beginning. It was never claimed that baptism is more, that it is the whole of Christian life in the continuing dynamic of man's relationship with God. It is claimed that baptism has lasting effects, that it effects a lasting mark or character, but the sacrament itself is received at a sacramental moment in a sacramental event. Much the same is true of other sacraments, but I question whether the "event" phenomenon is true of Holy Orders and matrimony.

Holy Orders is a sacrament that has always given theologians some difficulty in analyzing. It is not our purpose here to pursue that inquiry. But by way of observation, the Sacrament of Holy Orders suggests a dynamic of progression and continued growth in the service of God and pastoral care of the faithful, a living developmental sacrament that is never fully administered or fully received in a single sacramental event. I believe this thought should be investigated by theologians in order to discover if there is not some living sacramentality in the ministry of the Church. The Church itself is vital sacramental reality. What about the ministry?

Whatever the answer to the question of Holy Orders may be, I am thoroughly convinced that matrimony is a dynamic sacramental reality that is not fully received as a sacrament or fully expressed as a sign in any one sacramental event. I do not propose here to try to unfold the mystery of the sacrament. I do suggest that the Eastern Orthodox Church, which did not become paralyzed by the legalistic "consent-contract-bond" theology of marriage has a better appreciation of the dynamic reality of marriage as a life process. I believe, further, that Orthodox theology that was not confined by the legal concepts of the West, has maintained a more meaningful and dynamic sense of the sacramentality of matrimony.

The Eastern Christian Churches believe in the same sacramental signification of marriage; i.e., that the marital union is a sign of the union of Christ with the Church. The symbolization, however, does not have the clear, finished lines of a well-carved statue. Neither the marital union nor the union of Christ with his Church are accepted in Eastern thought as static, accomplished facts. Marital union is a living, constantly changing relationship which in life is either growing or diminishing. It is never static. The union of Christ with his Church is a transforming union, transforming human life and human history into the Kingdom of God—a kingdom that has not yet been realized, a kingdom that is yet to come through continuing redemption.

The Sacrament of Matrimony can be grasped only in terms of the signification of these two dynamic realities—the *living union* of spouses signifying the *transforming union* of Christ with his Church. Eastern theology views the sacramental reality of marriage as a total transforming of the total marital life through the continuing dynamic of the Kingdom of God being daily revealed and unfolded in Christian family and Christian community life. The "sign" of the sacrament cannot be captured in the stillness of the wedding portrait. It can only be seen in a movie.

The marriage ceremony in the Orthodox liturgy reflects symbolically the dynamism of the sacrament through the "movement" of the ritual. The couple to be married exchange vows in what amounts to a civil marriage ceremony conducted outside the main body of the church. Then a procession moves from the vestibule into the church and up to the sanctuary. This movement into the church symbolizes the transforming of the natural marriage into the spiritual dynamic of redemption and the building up of the Kingdom of God. The marriage is spiritually transformed not simply for the sake of human happiness on earth; but for the ultimate realization of the transcendent glory of the Eternal Christ and the Church Triumphant.

Eastern theology views the signification of the living union of spouses in a truly redemptive dimension. It sees the sacramental signification growing in life as there is born to the marital union ever deeper love and greater sharing of Christian life together. It also sees the signification diminish when spouses no longer share their life with a generous heart or constant will. It witnesses the death of the great mystery when partners no longer live in the union of love.

The Eastern Churches allow divorce when the lives of the spouses are no longer sacramental. The Orthodox Churches do not claim the power to dissolve marriage; but just as they witness the birth of sacramental marriages, they sadly admit that some of those unions die. They accept the reality that the Kingdom of God has not yet come, that the redeeming transformation is still taking place, that humanity is still weak and in need of mercy and forgiveness when it fails even in its most noble undertakings. George A. Maloney, S.J., after a review of the Orthodox position, suggests that the Church "has not the power to grant divorces; but it has the power to recognize by the Spirit, the bond of love and its sacramental absence where a marriage has ceased to be a true sacramental sign, not only signifying but also effecting what it signifies, the self-giving of Christ to His beloved spouse." ("Oeconomia: A Corrective to Law," *The Catholic Lawyer*, spring, 1971, p. 102.)

I believe that when the Roman Catholic Church won the battle of dogmatizing the law of indissolubility, it lost a sense of the dynamic mystery of sacramental marriage and it lost sight of the reality that some marriages die and dissolve of their own lifelessness and cease to be sacramental. I also believe that the Church can, without loss of doctrine or dignity, reclaim the mystery of the Sacrament of Matrimony and it can and should reclaim the mercy the Church should extend to her sons and daughters who fail through human weakness to show forth that mystery in their marriages. The price of reclaiming the Kingdom of Christ in marriage is to do away with the legalistic approach to the sacrament both in teaching and in the practice of the Curia and the tribunals. The reward will be the return of many tortured souls to communion with the Christian community through Eucharistic communion with Christ.

V

The Perfection of Marriage

Since marriage is more than a contract, the consummation of marriage involves more than the first act of carnal intercourse. Marriage is more than handing over the rights of the body for sexual acts apt to generate offspring. In the preceding chapter, the personal, social and sacramental dimensions of marriage were considered in their fruitfulness, faithfulness and lastingness. If we were to view marriage in its totality as a living, growing union in all its various dimensions, we would find that no marriage ever reaches total fullness or is completely consummated. The consummation or fullness of marriage may be considered under the following aspects. There are different kinds and varying degrees of consummation and fullness in marriage. Moreover, depending upon the degree and kind of consummation, the fullness may be momentary, fleeting, substantially lasting, almost permanently perfect. Total consummation of marriage is the full union of persons in which each person also reaches his own unique individual perfection. Total consummation of marriage does not occur this side of heaven. However, either a couple are continually striving for the total consummation of their marriage or they are moving away from it. In a sense, neither persons nor marriages ever stand still. They are growing or diminishing all the time.

In order for there to be a marriage, it must be consensual. The man and the woman must consent to marry each other. In my opinion, the beginning of the consummation of a marriage takes place when the man and the woman begin to realize, to be aware, that they are substantially attuned to each other psychologically and emotionally. It is in this latter awareness that they actually give themselves to each other as persons and grow in the giving. It is this emotional and psychological union that is the basic and primary consummation of marriage. Physical love-making is a most obvious and enjoyable sign of their giving of themselves to each other and receiving each other.

Granted the great importance of human physical love-making in most marriages and that two becoming one flesh can be a most human sign of mutual self-giving and other-receiving, marriage is first and essentially a union of persons, a mutual completion and complementation of persons as persons. This union is above all thoughtfully and consensually emotional and psychological. Unless a couple are united emotionally and psychologically, that is, unless they complete themselves and complement each other as alive human beings, it is likely that even a desirable and enjoyable physical complementation will become less and less pleasurable and may, in the face of a lack of personalness in other areas of life, become distasteful, unhealthy and perhaps even hateful. Over a period of time physical sex will ordinarily be increasingly enjoyable only to a couple who are alive to each other in the multitudinous other areas of personal union as well as within and because of the pressures of everyday living.

The mere fact of carnal copulation does not confirm and may not "perfect" the marriage in the slightest. It is absurd to say that Mary and Joseph were not fully and indissolubly married because they did not make love physically. It is equally absurd to say that most marriages between Catholics —simply most marriages—are not genuine marriages because in most marriages today at least one of the parties does not give to the other without reservation the right to sexual intercourse. This later conclusion, which derives from the present law of the Church, will be treated more completely when we consider the reasons for tribunal annulments.

The consensual consummation of a marriage takes place when a couple knowingly and willingly pledge themselves to a fruitful, lasting, mutual affection. This consensual consummation is externalized at the marriage ceremony. In fact, it may be months or years after the ceremony, after the marriage has been physically and psychologically consummated, that the couple will knowingly and willfully realize what they have pledged. This pledging is more of a mutual vowing than a bilateral contract. Neither the fulfillment of the pledges or vows of marriage nor the consummation of marriage can be framed in the words or concepts of a contract in the ordinary sense of the word.

The overemphasis of the Catholic Church on the initial act of marital intercourse has been brought home to me many times by the stories married couples tell of their first act or attempted act of physical love-making. Sometimes it is wonderful. At other times it is painful to one or the other or to both. At least now and again it is for one or the other selfish rather than self-giving. Too often it is impersonal for one or the other. There are couples who, the next day or years following their marriage, will laugh at the ridiculousness of their first attempt to make love with each other. How often have I heard women say that they came home from their honeymoons crying to their mothers about "the horrible thing he tried to do to me"? Fortunately, the mother and the family doctor explained the sexual facts of life to these women in such a way that they were able to enjoy them. And then there are the sad cases, more than a few, where one party was puzzled, frustrated, amazed and angry that the other party did not try to do anything or would not permit anything to be done.

And how long it took me and other tribunal priests to learn the chasm between the questions: "When did you first have intercourse with your husband?" and "When did you and your husband first make love?" And it took an even longer time for me to realize that the answer to either question was none of my business. Nor should it be the business of the Church. The first and essential union of marriage is a personal union, a union of personal love. The "personalness" of the human love relationship should be respected—completely respected. The Church need only witness the pledge to know that the marriage has been made. It need not know and has no business investigating how or when that personal union was consummated.

Marriage does have a social dimension and the married couple do have social obligations. Marriage involves civil effects of individuals' property, inheritance, the good of the children, the welfare of their family in the civil society as well as the broader civil concerns of the general population and economy affected by family life. Civil law is necessarily concerned with the social dimension of the fruitfulness, faithfulness and lastingness of marriage. Since the social dimension of marriage involves a complex relationship of moral rights and moral obligations not only between the couple themselves, between parents and children, but between family and civil society, the Church must be concerned with guiding marriage toward moral perfection in the social order.

Marriage is consummated in its social dimension when the couple embrace their moral responsibility in society as married partners. Social consummation is effected by any and every action that tends toward fulfilling their moral responsibility to society. This could involve anything from the decision to have or not to have children to the use of their mutual possessions for the welfare of the aged. Whatever they do as a married couple and/or as a family to enhance the community, to enrich the society in a real sense consummates and perfects their union in its social dimension.

Marriage in its sacramental dimension is consummated whenever it shows forth a fruitful, faithful, lasting union of love as a sign of the union of Christ with the Church. As a sacrament, marriage extends the personal dimension to include the mutual assistance of each spouse to attain eternal salvation; it extends the social dimension to so serve in the Christian community that it in turn is a redeeming factor in the world, that it continues generation after generation to strive to restore all things in Christ. As Vatican II clearly pointed out, it is the laity—the married couple, the family—who are most suited to the task of serving as leaven in the world.

The Church then must be especially concerned with the perfection, the consummation, of marriage in its sacramental dimension, because that consummation is identical with the purpose and ideals of its mission in the world. The Church must educate and motivate young couples to so love one another that they will, through their union, perfect love in its personal, social and sacramental dimensions. This is the one consuming ideal toward which the Church should turn its attention and its efforts with regard to marriage.

There may have been a time in history when there was a valid argument for teaching the ideals of marriage through the prescriptions of law and the force of penalty. To attempt the same thing today is utterly devoid of reason. Even if the law were respected today, law is not an acceptable way of "teaching" in our society. And if law were respected and the law were an acceptable way of teaching, present law would be inadequate to the task. It is antiquated, narrow and unjust. The present law is too unrealistic to grasp the meaning of love in all its dimensions, to appreciate love's ideal of fruitfulness, faithfulness and lastingness, or to grant mercy when love's ideals are not attained.

The Church's task is to teach and guide and assist human beings struggling for the ideal and to help them pick up the pieces when they fail. To be able to balance the highest of ideals with the facts of total failure, the Church must be totally realistic at all times. It must be totally realistic in the ideals it teaches its members and it must be totally realistic when it faces the failures some of its children make of their matches.

*

There has never been an ideal, model marriage in the history of mankind. There has never been the ideal, model man born of human wedlock. There has never been the ideal, model family. Of course, it is sometimes said that the marriage of St. Joseph and the Blessed Virgin Mary was the model marriage and that the model home was that of the Holy Family. There is a great deal of truth for Catholics in this notion of the ideals of Joseph and Mary, but their marriage could hardly be the model of perfect marriage relationship, nor is the Holy Family the model of Christian family life. We believe, of course, that thoughtfulness, tenderness, mutual love and affection and total self-giving marked the marriage of Joseph and Mary. In the personal dimension each became a fuller person because of their love for each other, and in its social dimension and sacramental dimension their marriage and their home played a providential role in the redemption of mankind. They provided for the birth, the care and protection of the Savior in the early years of His mission. In these and other ways their marriage shows forth many of the ideals for all married couples. But as a model of other marriages? No. In Divine Providence their marriage was unique—so unique it could never be a model on which others might pattern their own ideal of marriage.

I would hold that their marriage was consummated in its personal, social and sacramental dimensions, without physical intercourse. Because it was and remained a virginal relationship, I would say that it is not the model of Christian marital love. The offspring was not born of the wedlock, and although the foster home was the first "Christian home," it is not the model of other Christian homes where the children are of the one flesh of man and wife in physical union.

It seems strange and unrealistic that the marriage of Joseph and Mary, which is devotionally set before Catholics as a model of perfection because of the purity of the spouses' love, is, according to a weird involution of the law, not a consummated marriage. In the present law and practice of the Church such a marriage could be dissolved due to the lack of perfection. The marriage was not consummated in the way required by law—physical intercourse. I cannot accept the law or the conclusion of the law in this matter. I believe the marriage of Joseph and Mary was really consummated in the personal union that expressed most of the ideals of marriage. Because it does stand so uniquely in the history of human relationships, however, it is no model for other marriages.

To search for a unique model is a useless enterprise. On the other hand, an ideal marriage may be no further than your neighbors' next door. It may even be closer to home than that, if you look, not with stars in your eyes or with idle fantasies playing in the imagination, but with the realism that sees the ideal marriage as the union of two persons trying to live together as one—trying to share a common life of mutual affection. To set the ideal of marriage at some unobtainable level of perfection is not to have an ideal at all. The ideal must be, for the most part, obtainable in the realistic order or it is not an ideal but an idle dream. I believe that a great many, perhaps most marriages—Christian or not—attain a remarkable measure of the realistic ideal. And I believe that many couples are living in an ideal or very close to ideal marriage on this earth, but do not realize it because the ideals they have learned of what human love can attain in life are unrealistic. I believe that the problems and difficulties they meet are not always due to a lack of their commitment to a shared life. It may be that most of their difficulties arise from the very fact that they are sharing deeply the sufferings that are common to the human condition. The ideal marriage is not a romantic romp through life without problems, without pain, without difficulty of any kind. The ideal marriage is one in which the couple meet and work with and even suffer their difficulties together. The ideal marriage begins with an infant love, which with mutual care grows to maturity in meeting the responsibility and suffering the consequences of living in this world as one.

If the church is to play a realistic role in helping couples attain Christian ideals in marriage, the Church must be soberly realistic in its teaching regarding marriage ideals. It must be just as soberly realistic in bringing not only justice to its legislation regarding the effects of marriage, but also mercy to the parties who must continue to live beyond the disaster of broken marriage. The need today is for a better preparation for and more perseverance in marriage. The Church should here play a vital educational and counseling role through a realistic teaching regarding marriage with realistic laws regarding the social and sacramental dimensions of marriage.

VI

Preparation for and Perseverance in Marriage

Thirty years or so ago, in the early 1940s, there was the beginning of an attempt on the part of the Church in the United States to present a positive program of preparation for couples planning marriage. The Archdioceses of Chicago and Newark were the forerunners of this movement. While this was, in large part, a passive program for the couples, they were the recipients of information about marriage from married couples, doctors and priests. This information many of them would not have received in a clear and healthy manner because of their sexually inhibited homes. These marriage forums, or Pre-Cana Conferences as they later came to be called, did and do serve a purpose. Initially, the late Monsignor Charles Walsh and Monsignor George A. Kelly were largely responsible for their success in New York. I worked with Monsignor Walsh and Monsignor Kelly in these programs. In the course of the years, there was more active participation on the part of the couples with the "teachers" in the program and more open and frank discussion among the participants themselves. These programs still exist in most places in the United States and, at least in a numerical sense, are flourishing.

There are a number of puzzling features about these programs. The mood of passivity about them, the lack of genuine life, the absence of dynamic interchange creates the feeling that there is something unreal about the whole preparatory process. Couples who have had similar programs in high school or college are often bored by them. Couples who seem most in need of preparation for marriage either do not attend the programs or attend with closed minds if not closed ears. Some couples are hurt by the hostility generated when they are compelled by Church law to attend.

In my twelve years in these programs I do not recall even

one couple who stopped going together because of their experience at the conferences. I consider this a negative criticism of the program since one of its primary purposes should have been to alert couples to be psychologically or emotionally aware of each other as persons—their similarities, their differences, their deficiencies and their good points. Some couples faithfully attended these conferences but their marriages were immediate and total disasters. In spite of the preparatory courses not one of these couples had a sense of impending disaster before they married. As one woman put it, "When love is in bloom before marriage, the couple idealize each other to the point where no one can touch them or reach them." They are living in their dream world. Many of them find the journey of going together better than the destination of marriage. They were unable to grapple with postmarital problems because such problems, if considered at all, seemed so remote that they were not prepared to cope with them.

As I knew the marriage preparation courses years ago, there was too much emphasis, on one hand, upon the negative and restrictive aspects of physical sex and, on the other, upon the lofty and often unrealistic religious ideal of marriage.

Sex education was as excessively puritanical as marriage education was legalistic. The moralists became expert in the mathematics of measuring exactly how many inches above a given hemline or below a given neckline constituted a venial sin of immodesty, a proximate occasion of serious sin, or a mortal sin of indecent exposure. Even the moralists were confused by the calculus of kissing, and determining the degrees of venereal pleasure in touching defied the most astute in geometry. All of this would be hilarious if it had not caused so much unnecessary sense of guilt, neurotic tendencies, bizarre pseudo-sexual acts and, may God forgive us, psychoses or psychotic episodes. The fact is that we did raise up a generation of fathers and mothers with large sexual hang-ups.

Young people today do not see the suffering, the frustrations, the torment of the former generation, but they see the absurdity of its teaching, if only in the light of the biology of sex. At least biology is the science of the living, but the biological approach to sex also falls short of conveying a genuine appreciation of human sexuality. The decision of educators, including many Catholic educators, to go biological in sex education at an early age has certain merits in avoiding the attitude of other generations that sex is shameful at best, and sinful in every way with the exception of the sexual act in marriage. The dangers in the biological approach are that sex becomes a thing unto itself, that sexual satisfaction is basically a biological function of the body, that substantial sexual satisfaction can be obtained in the sexual acts that are transient. These are the dangers, too, that biological sexual activity can be manipulated without further moral or social responsibility, that the physical and superficially emotional aspects of sex are given a higher place in human living and personal fulfillment than the total self-giving, self-sacrificing mutual affection between a man and a woman.

That this biological approach with its behavioral conclusions has had a tremendous influence in our present society should be obvious to anyone who passes a newsstand or makes the mistake of going to a massage parlor for a massage. The majority of young people today, however, have not been fooled. In spite of the sexual hang-ups of their priests and their parents and in spite of the exploiters of the streets, many young people today do not find sin in every sign of premarital and postmarital affection, nor are they foolish enough to seek personal fulfillment in licentious sexuality.

Without the aid of the Church and the home, without the license of the streets, many young couples have come to rather mature conclusions about what they expect of life and about a responsible way to go about achieving their expectations by sharing their lives together. They do not consider sex shameful or sinful, but neither are they preoccupied with sex as the total or even central concern of life. This attitude is evident in the growing personalism that is emerging as the characteristic of the new generation. The Church, parents, educators must grasp the meaning of this age. They must grasp the balance and the realism of the position and give their teaching, their counseling, their laws the same realism and balance.

In the meantime, many people, especially young couples,

are left without realistic guidance. They cannot wait until the Church in its official teaching and its laws catches up with common sense. Hopefully, there will be enough priests, parents, educators to assist the young along the line of mature, responsible attitudes about sex and marriage, and there will be sufficient realistic counseling regarding the normal expectations of life in this world and the expectations of marriage in particular.

There must be more emphasis on the development of personal maturity in education. The basic psychological and emotional factors in personality development and fulfillment are more important here than the intellectual and physical development which has been the traditional task of education and training. Personal maturity is the foundation of marriage and that personal maturity cannot be measured by intellectual perspicacity or the polish of physical skills. The poor, disadvantaged couple in Appalachia with as little formal education as property may be psychologically and emotionally more mature for their marriage than the star football player and queen of the graduating class of the state university. Whatever helps to develop personal maturity from the earliest ages of childhood is remote preparation for marriage.

Sex education should begin early in the home and in formal education of the schools. It should be directed toward the role of sexuality in total personality development and should not dwell on the negative prohibitions of isolated physical sexual acts nor in the biology of physical sexuality. The most important factor in preparation for marriage is that the man and woman each have a sense of their own personal dignity and worth, a sense of at least the initial fullness and completeness of themselves as persons. The dignity of the unique individual person—whether baptized or not—is prior to the dignity of the couple united in marriage. Unless each person has and enhances in marriage his or her individual personality, there will be no growth in dignity; there will simply be no growth in the couple as a couple.

When a young man and young woman begin seriously to think of marriage they should already have reached a certain maturity of personality so that they have some realistic notion of what they expect in life and what they expect in a married partner. Hopefully, this expectation will help them discern a likely partner, before the "love bug" renders them hopelessly incapable of mature discernment.

When two young people are seriously considering marriage they should make every effort to see each other as "real persons" not as love objects. If the couple are of different religions—or if one is religious and one is not—it is essential that they discuss the difference openly as to the effect it will have on their individual lives and their life as a couple. A person, man or woman, who compromises basic religious belief in the hope of having or making peace in marriage is a victim of self-delusion. Dedication to religion is an integral dimension of the human person. If anyone diminishes this dedication in a substantial way, he diminishes himself as a person.

Whenever it is possible, it is important that the couple not only know each other well and appreciate each other as persons but that they know each other's families and like and appreciate them. At times, the inability of a person to feel at home before marriage with the family of the person he or she is thinking of marrying may be a sign that the displeasing qualities of the family have not surfaced in the other person. The least that should be done is to bring the problem out in the open, to discuss frankly the reasons for the problem and to decide upon straightforward solutions. No problem is solved—it is often aggravated—by the statement, "It will work out all right after we are married."

Thoughtfulness and tenderness—in words, in gift remembrances on important occasions and in signs of physical affection—are two of the more important components of marriage for each and both parties. Indications of a lack of continued thoughtfulness and tenderness before marriage are very dangerous signals. These qualities are not likely to be created anew after marriage, and without them a marriage can be a disaster. Either or both parties—as well as the children in a marriage—can be hurt badly. The beautiful expressions about thoughtfulness and tenderness expressed in the Song of Songs in the Old Testament and in the thirteenth chapter of Paul's First Letter to the Corinthians in the New Testament would well be read individually and together, and talked about by engaged and married couples.

Each person going into any marriage has unique virtues, deficiencies, good and bad habits. A couple planning marriage would do well to search out these qualities in each other. They should talk frankly about them. They should try to find out if each can benefit from the virtues of the other, if the deficiencies and bad habits of one can be compensated for, and perhaps be eliminated by the virtues and good habits of the other. If there are signs of problems in these areas—or in the inability of one or both persons to get along with the family of the other—it would be well if the couple spoke for a couple of hours with a marriage counselor who is a professional psychologist or psychiatrist.

While equality of persons—all persons as persons—should be a fact in all areas of life, a man considering marriage should be very alert that the woman of his choice is all person because she is all woman. A woman should be alert that the man of her choice is all man. In the total person of a woman and in the total person of a man there are differences and contrasts as basic, although not always as obvious, as their biological differences and contrasts. If a man and a woman about to marry do not see these differences as contrasting, and in some ways contradictory, their intended marriage could be headed for trouble. It is these differences and contrasts that draw a man and a woman to complete themselves as persons in marriage and to complement themselves as a couple.

Beyond setting requirements for age and mandating that one person in the marriage be a man and the other a woman, neither the Church nor the state can legislate effectively on the requirements for a lawful marriage. The state, and especially churches and other religious communities can increase the number of marriages that are initially good and can increase the stability of the marriage state by realistically setting forth, and explaining positively that the dignity of the person, the dignity of the couple and the good of the community call for tenderness, thoughtfulness, faithfulness, lastingness, fruitfulness in marriage.

In most marriages, perseverance will require something

akin to a gentle persistence during the tolerable and intolerable periods that occur in every marriage. Once the honeymoon is over, there will be tolerable periods and at least some intolerable days even in the most enjoyable of marriages. The best suggestion that can be made to couples in marriage is that they try to follow the advice given by doctors, married couples, spiritual leaders and professional counselors to couples before marriage. Married couples will meet, run into, and sometimes be overrun by problems. They will cope with the problems only if they face the problems immediately and grapple with them directly. If they do not or are unable to cope with a problem quickly and successfully, they should speak with a psychologist or a psychiatrist, not with their relatives or friends.

The partners in marriage should never belittle themselves or their mate as persons. Moreover, the kind word when there is no obligation to say it, the thoughtful gift when there is no special occasion for it, the tender touch when the other person needs it—gestures such as these, done sometimes easily and sometimes with a swallowing of what is often false pride, will go a long way toward keeping joy and happiness in a marriage.

If a couple enter into the marital union as whole persons attuned to the personality of each other with a will to molding their personalities into a oneness of life, many of the responsibilities and results of the social and sacramental dimensions of their marriage will be met and achieved and many of the problems overcome with relative ease and without a great deal of outside help or counseling. In the social and sacramental dimensions, however, married couples must relate to other parties interested in the success or failure of their union and in its effect on the welfare of the community. There is a need for marriage law both for the welfare of the civic community and the religious community. My own deep concern is that the marriage law of the Church be radically revised to serve the welfare of the religious community, the civic community and the couples of every marriage. In order to do that, the Church must first recognize the dignity of every human person in its marriage law. We have seen in this chapter that every marriage rests on respect for the dignity of the human persons entering into the marital union. Every good law concerning marriage must have the same basis.

VII

The Importance of Good Marriage Laws

Over the years my work with the tribunal made me increasingly aware that, in practice, the Catholic Church does not recognize the basic equality of all persons as persons. In the substantive and procedural laws of the tribunal there is a distinct gradation of persons. This gradation, from inferiority to superiority, might be listed as follows: unbaptized persons, baptized non-Catholics, Catholic women, Catholic men, priests, bishops and pope. These different groups exist in the Church aside from goodness or lack of same, ability or lack of same, intelligence or lack of same. This dignity and rank is not simply ascribed to the office or to the responsibility attached to an office. Personal intelligence and personal ability, if not personal honesty, integrity and moral goodness, are presumed to be present in a higher degree in the pope than in bishops; in bishops, than in priest; in priests, than in laity. Moral goodness is not presumed in the same way and to the same degree. Distrust of the laity is only thinly veiled; e.g., lack of honesty is implied in the parties and witnesses for the annulment or dissolution of a marriage.

The manner of exercising authority in the Church is often insulting to the intelligence of the subjects seeking justice and judgment. The exercise of power without giving reasons for the action or the reversal of decisions without explanation can do nothing but convey the impression to intelligent people that the power was exercised without reason and decisions are completely arbitrary. Censorship, although changed with regard to the Index of Forbidden Books, is a common practice in many curial procedures, and secrecy is the weapon used to protect the innocent from scandal.

In short, much of the law and legal procedures in the Church continue to reflect the presumed superiority of the hierarchy, who, schooled in divine revelation, were believed to be possessed of intelligence, wisdom and prudence, beyond the measure of the hordes of infidels and the herds of peasants within their pastoral domain. This superiority supposedly justified the use of power without explanation, guaranteed to the ignorant justice without recourse, and protected the innocent from the scandal of procedures and decisions they would not understand. There still seems to be in high places some who believe that in the pagan world of today, that in a world so given over to evil and to error, the Church alone possesses the truth, the Church alone possesses the power, and the Church alone in its wisdom and power is able to judge the nations. It is a doctrine of the Dark Ages.

This attitude enjoyed a particularly triumphant throne in the provisions of the Code of Canon Law governing marriage. The Church was for many the last remaining fortress in the world for the protection of the indissolubility of marriage and for the protection of the family. Yet it was apparent to me, working in the tribunal, that the Church was maintaining the castle at the cost of destroying the dignity of the human person. And because it would cost them their dignity, fewer and fewer persons were coming to the castle or seeking protection within the fortress. The law and the tribunal are the last remaining fortresses. They were built for another time. The inhabitants of land, the ignorant infidel, the simple peasant and the lowly vassal, have moved to another time and place. They have found their God-given dignity as persons and they will not recross the mote to seek refuge in the past.

It would be unfair to label the law of the Church developed during the Middle Ages and even later as the work of pompous arrogance. Actually, the Church did much in the thirteenth and sixteenth centuries to promote equal treatment to the sexes and to bring equal justice to slaves, at least with regard to marriage and family. But such triumph has passed away and now the law of the Church must not remain entrenched in the past. It must build anew on the very basis of individual human dignity and the equality of persons as persons before God, before the Church and before the State which it championed in other ways. We will not begin to realize how very little we have done in this regard or how rightly and how far the Protestant and secular world has passed us by until we seriously attempt to correct the law. It is particularly important to begin this reform in the area of marriage legislation: first, because it has caused and is causing now more human anguish and greater injustice to more people than any other area of Church law; secondly, because it is perhaps the most degrading segment of the Code of Canon Law with regard to basic human dignity and rights; and, thirdly, if we are to restore people to the Church, we must restore the Church to the people through renewed understanding and practice regarding marriage and the family.

*

It is most important that a person have a sense of his unique dignity and worth because he is a person. The unique dignity of a person grows and thrives best by reason of personal contact with other persons. With the great majority of persons in the world this uniqueness of personality matures best in marriage, the most intimate of personal contacts. Ideally, and very realistically, as a man and a woman in marriage complete each other physically, emotionally, psychologically, mentally and spiritually, the unique personality of each of them grows apace. The uniqueness of each of them and their completion of each other, their fruitfulness for and with each other has its impact upon the community in which they live and work. The uniqueness of each of them and their complementation of each other fosters dignity in each of them as individuals and as a couple. These qualities, in turn, highlight the God-given worth of their children, their relatives and their neighbors.

The awareness of the personal dignity of all individuals makes healthy married couples intolerant of ill-informed and indiscriminate judgment of any person regardless of religion, race or color. Because personal unselfishness is a large dimension of their uniqueness as individuals and as a couple, couples today, especially the young, instinctively reject any false superiority and authoritarianism—religious or otherwise. They find unsupportable the cold, impersonal resolution of social problems such as poverty or racism. Injustice in any form, punishment which is not remedial, anonymous or indirect judgments are abhorrent. Many today, especially the young, are eagerly open to learning from any other person or experience or community. The uniqueness of their freedom as individuals and as couples makes them more sensitive to the freedom and rights of others and loathe to assume bad motives in each other or any other persons. They prefer, to the old hang-ups, simply to let it all hang out. Their freedom fosters in them the sense that laws must be good and must be applied humanly if there is to be a healthy social order in civil and religious communities.

There is great value in the fresh, frank approach to all matters of human relationships. I see the need for the same kind of fresh, frank and open approach to a renewal of law. It seems that a genuine renewal in law could be brought about by awakening a more acute awareness of the worth and dignity of the individual person and the worth and dignity of the community of persons.

My first substantial attempt to participate in the renewal of the law of the Catholic Church was concerned with an overall approach to the revision of canon law with a few recommendations directed specifically at marriage legislation. My recommendations to the members of the Canon Law Society of America at the annual meeting of the Society in Chicago in 1964 were unanimously approved by that group. With the technical legal language put into plain English and with some explanatory phrases added, the recommendations read substantially as follows:

1. That there be a re-evaluation of the nature and purpose of the law of the Catholic Church insofar as it tends to perfect the People of God.

2. That in this re-evaluation there be an awareness of the current scriptural and theological clarifications of the nature and mission of the Church, as well as an awareness of the need for Church lawyers to be familiar with the secular sciences; e.g., psychology, which contribute to the making of good law.

3. That charity and a compassionate concern for persons be strong motivating factors in the formulation of

the law; e.g., the laws concerning Christian burial, laws affecting persons who are not Catholics.

4. That, in addition to the concepts of Roman law, the concepts of Germanic, Anglo-American, Oriental and civil law be considered in the formulation of the revised Code of Canon Law.

5. That there be a careful scrutiny of those laws which were formulated in the historical context of violent conflict with Jews, Protestants, Orthodox and/or other religious or secular bodies insofar as these laws indicated a lack of justice and a lack of charity.

6. That it be clearly stated that persons who were not baptized in the Catholic Church, or who were not converted to the Catholic Faith, are not subject to the laws of the Catholic Church.

7. That the content and terminology of the law be formulated with the strong presumption that all persons, Catholic and other than Catholic, are persons of integrity, good character and honest conscience, and that their word is trustworthy.

8. That the objections to the laws of the Church by persons who are not Catholic be thoughtfully considered, inasmuch as these objections may point to a lack of justice, equity or charity in the law.

9. That penal laws be drastically curtailed and simplified and that their application be placed in the hands of the local bishops or regional and national conferences of bishops and that they be personally imposed.

10. That a person accused of violating Church law be not punished unless he is aware of the nature of the accusation, the identity of his accuser, the evidence adduced to substantiate the truth of the accusation; that he have sufficient time and adequate professional assistance to defend himself; that he be presumed innocent unless the contrary is proven beyond reasonable doubt.

11. That wherever possible decisions, permissions and delegations of authority now reserved to the pope or the Commissions of Congregations in Rome, be transferred

to local bishops or other persons or organizations—
including lay persons—in the Church.

12. That the safeguarding of the rights of persons be
at least on a par with the safeguarding of the dignity of
the sacraments.

13. That the rights and interests of priests and religious, along with those of pastors and superiors, be
clearly stated, upheld and safeguarded.

14. That the rights of women be equal with the rights
of men.

15. That very serious consideration be given to the
fact that, under the present laws of the tribunal, persons
seeking annulments or dissolutions (divorces) of marriages often suffer grave injustices inasmuch as they do
not have adequate opportunity to vindicate their rights
or to seek relief in the present law.

16. That the rights and interests of lay persons be
clearly stated, upheld and safeguarded.

17. That the freedom of conscience of the individual
person be respected and safeguarded; e.g., in laws concerning the writing, prohibition and censure of books.

18. That the work and experience of the United Nations and the World Council of Churches be taken into
consideration in the formulation of the new law.

Eight years later, I would make only a few changes in most
of the resolutions, including these: (1) that there should be
as few specific or statute laws as possible, and (2) that laws
be local or regional rather than universal.

The guiding principle in every one of the recommendations
is the assertion and safeguarding of the dignity of the human
person. The application of this principle to marriage law was
my greatest concern, and these general recommendations
were not specific enough.

There was further need to make explicit the reforms implied in Number 15 of the recommendations. A step in that
direction was taken in the modification of the procedural laws
of the tribunal when, on July 1, 1970, the twenty-three rules
of procedure, called the "American Norms," were approved

for the Church in the United States for a three-year "trial" period.* Much of the anonymity and impersonality of the tribunal procedures were at least temporarily relieved in the United States.

The nature and effect of these procedural norms will be discussed later. The issue here is that the Church law has not been radically changed by the introduction of these norms.†

The very relaxing of the procedural rules in the United States has gradually served to highlight the lack of realism in the substantive marriage law of the Church. Now there are many—lay people and clergy—who question the value of the Church tribunal in the entire area of annulments and divorces.

The basic disorder of present marriage law remains. It is not the function of law to teach moral ideals, but to attend to justice and order in the community with due regard for the dignity and rights of the individuals. Further, there is need for the Church to face frankly and directly and realistically the problem of the intolerable marriage.

No matter how good the remote and proximate preparation for marriage, no matter how well the law provides for the social and sacramental dimensions of successful marriages, the fact is that some marriages will fail. The law must deal with failure as honestly, as realistically, as justly as it does with success. The present manner in which the Church handles the intolerable marriage is unrealistic and unjust, a needless cause of unusual suffering, and often degrading to the dignity of the persons who have been caught in a human tragedy.

---

* On June 20, 1973, the "America Norms" were extended for one year. On June 29, 1974, they were extended indefinitely.
† On October 1, 1971, in a document entitled "Matrimonial Causes," Pope Paul VI made some changes in the procedural law for the universal Church. These changes did not eliminate the substantial deficiencies in the procedural law. Moreover, no changes were made in the substantive law; that is, in the reasons why marriages are annulled or dissolved.

VIII

The Intolerable Marriage and the Tribunal

There is no question but that Our Lord taught the indissolubility of marriage as a quality of every marriage. There is no question that the ideal of marriage is the union of one man and one woman who, in an exchange of marital affection, vow to be lovingly faithful to each other until death and look forward to the bearing and bringing up of children as part of the fruitfulness of their marriage. This is ordinarily the ideal concept of marriage in at least all of the major religions in the Western world.

It is also a fact that life in this world is a bittersweet pilgrimage with a mixture of joy and sorrow sometimes so intertwined that they seem indistinguishable one from the other. It is very, very often a fact of life that, with or without guilt or any direct intention, couples who marry fail to attain the ideal marriage. The spouses fail in some measure to help each other grow, or somehow fail to grow together, to be constantly or lastingly faithful to each other.

There is a sad wistfulness in a marriage that is only tolerable. It means that either or both of the partners have been unable or unwilling to give themselves utterly to each other. Perhaps they are unwilling or unable, or afraid, to take the chance of finding out that basically they may be intolerable to each other in marriage.

Any marriage in this real world is at times and on occasion only intolerable. Every marriage, if the persons are truly trying to be alive and to grow as individuals by growing up and into each other, is at times intolerable. It may happen that the very intolerable moments in a marriage are the occasions that ultimately spark and nourish marital affection. Peace at any price, in marriage as well as in war, and in every form of living, is diminishing, deadening and destructive. A consistently tolerable marriage, if it does not drive a man and woman to drink, drugs or other illusory substitutes for happiness, will certainly never change the face of even the little earth in which they live. Any time a husband and wife cannot look at each other nakedly—eyeball to eyeball—and be nakedly truthful to and with each other even when it means a hostile confrontation, their marriage has taken a step backwards. They begin to be reserved in their giving and selfish as well as self-serving in their taking.

In a good many instances the joy of a marriage will diminish and disappear. When this happens the marriage may or may not remain tolerable. If it comes to the point that one party is sick of the other or the couple are sick of each other, if it comes to the point that one party can't stand the other or the couple can't stand each other, the marriage is no longer tolerable. If the couple have taken all the means they are able or willing to take to recover a new beginning of marital affection and have failed to do so, the marriage has become irreparably and irrevocably intolerable. The marriage is dead. Every failure to live up to the ideal is a tragedy. A few persons of heroic stature may be able to grow with such a tragedy. These heroic persons are a sign of man's ability, with God's help, to do what for others would be humanly impossible. Their heroism, if it is that, is a sign of fortitude. It is not a sign of marriage.

The absolutism of the Church, when she states that all marriages, no matter how dead they may obviously be, are signs of Christ's Living Presence in the world, is woefully misplaced. We have discussed the weakness of the theological, or doctrinal, position of the Church regarding the sacramentality of marriage in another chapter. This weakness is nowhere more evident than in the face of an intolerable marriage.

Neither preparation for marriage nor marriage itself nor the life or death of a marriage can be legislated by statute law. Persons may be led or drawn—perhaps even coaxed—into healthy and wholesome marriages. Persons cannot be forced or pressured or legislated into good marriages. Those unfortunate couples who experience a broken marriage cannot be forced or pressured or legislated into making their relationship into a sign of Christ's love for and unity with the

Church. People cannot be forced into continuing in a sick or dead relationship. Couples do break up—sometimes for their own good, sometimes for the good of the children—they stop living with each other; they get a civil divorce to effect property arrangements and child care—the marriage ceases to exist in any discernible way.

Yet the Church teaches that the marriage still exists in its full natural and/or sacramental effect as if the natural or sacramental bond was some third thing with an independent, living entity which exists in its own right apart from the dead relationship of the two people who have gone their separate ways. The Church's response to the intolerable marriage is that it must protect this third thing, and it does so with a set of laws and legal structures designed to defend the existence of the bond unless it can be proven beyond doubt that the bond never existed or in some way lacks perfection either because at least one of the spouses was not baptized or the union was not physically consummated.

This is no response to the intolerable marriage at all. Baptism or non-baptism is not going to make an intolerable marriage one bit more tolerable; one act of intercourse more or less is not going to make an intolerable marriage a loving or lasting union. If the marriage was validly entered and was both sacramental and consummated, the Church says it is absolutely indissoluble and neither one of the separated couple of such an intolerable marriage can marry anyone else until the death of the former mate. There is no possible recourse in the law or in the tribunal procedures for such cases. If a person from such a broken marriage should attempt to remarry, the second marriage is invalid, and if the second couple should cohabit and for as long as they dare to continue living with each other, they are considered to be living in a state of mortal sin. They are considered public sinners. They are forbidden to receive Holy Communion. In the logic of Church law, they are presumed to be on the road to hell.

Although the Church does not really have a wholesome response to the intolerable marriage, it does happen that couples who find their marriages intolerable may also find there is a legal channel open for the dissolution of the marriage or that there may be grounds for an annulment. If dissolution or annulment is possible, the case will be processed in the tribunals established by the Church for this purpose. The tribunal is the Church court through which a Catholic may be declared free of a first marriage and may lawfully marry a second time and continue to be a Catholic in good standing. One who has used the tribunal to obtain a dissolution (divorce) or annulment may take active part in the Eucharistic celebration by receiving Holy Communion and is accepted in the Catholic community without any stigma attached to the failure of the first marriage.

Those who have evident grounds for a dissolution or annulment may have their cases processed in a reasonable length of time and without demeaning the former or intended spouses. But the tribunal procedures in difficult cases can be insufferable. To review the procedure will have some value, but it must be remembered that each diocesan tribunal is the creation of the bishop and may or may not conform to the standard of operation discussed here.

*

A person, Catholic or other than Catholic, may seek a Catholic annulment of his marriage in the diocese in which he resides or in the diocese in which he was married. When a person seeks an annulment, he or she makes an appointment—usually at the tribunal—with an advocate, a priest, who will be the person's lawyer in the course of the proceedings. An appointment may be made through a parish priest or by telephoning the administrative offices or the tribunal of the diocese or archdiocese.

If the advocate does not think the person has a basis for an annulment, the person may ask for another advocate. If the advocate thinks there may be a case for an annulment, he will gather whatever documents—civil, ecclesiastical, medical—are necessary to support the petition. He will hold preliminary interviews with each party to the marriage and possibly some of the potential witnesses in order to clarify the grounds for the annulment. He will then have the person present a petition stating the reasons and grounds for an annulment to the presiding judge of the tribunal. If the petition is rejected, the person may have recourse to a tribunal of appeal. For example, the tribunal of Philadelphia is the tribunal of appeal for the tribunal of New York. Ordinarily, the presiding judge with two other judges will be responsible for rendering the trial decision. Once a petition is accepted for processing, a member of the court called the defender of the marriage bond, the equivalent of a civil district attorney or prosecuting attorney, enters the scene. The judge takes the testimony of the parties and the other witnesses involved, and obtains further documentation if necessary; the advocate for the petitioner—the other party may also have an advocate—and the defender of the bond will, respectively, seek to muster arguments in favor of and against the annulment.

If necessary, the judge may call for the opinions of medical or other expert witnesses. When all of the available testimony and documentary evidence has been gathered, the advocate and the defender of the bond will present written statements summarizing their positions. The three judges will then review the evidence and the briefs of the advocate and the defender of the bond, and render a decision.

If the decision is negative, the petitioner may appeal to the tribunal of appeal. Once a negative decision has been given, two affirmative decisions are required to reverse it. Ordinarily, the first tribunal of appeal is the tribunal of a neighboring diocese, the second tribunal of appeal is the Roman Rota. If the decision is affirmative, the defender of the bond must appeal. If the affirmative decision is reversed in appeal, the case may go to the Roman Rota where the decision will be final.

If the defender of the bond appeals against an affirmative decision, the petitioner may ask the ordinary tribunal of appeal to uphold the initial affirmative decision. If the tribunal of appeal seconds the affirmative decision, and the defender of the bond does not appeal, the parties are free to remarry in the Church. Rarely will the defender of the bond in the tribunal of appeal call into question two consecutive affirmative decisions. But if he felt justified to appeal the case to the Roman Rota, the decision of Rome would be final.

With the approval of the American Norms, some changes in the procedure are temporarily in effect. For example, in the temporary norms there may be one judge instead of three; any person regardless of sex, religion or apparent guilt or lack of responsibility, may introduce a case in the diocese or archdiocese of his residence, in a diocese where witnesses may be more easily contacted, or in the diocese where the marriage was contracted; one affirmative decision given by one court may be acted upon immediately, without appeal; the rights of the lawyers of the parties are on a par with those of the defender of the bond. Further, the procedure may not be voided by some minor violation of the law. In short, these temporary norms introduced a measure of due process and justice badly lacking in the Code of Canon Law.

Whether the American Norms remain in effect or our tribunals will be directed to return to the universal law of the Church, the fact remains that the tribunals in the United States do not function uniformly. The results of a petition will in large measure depend on the diocese in which the case is processed.

When a person lives in a diocese in which the tribunal does not function—or functions only minimally—he should immediately, and I mean immediately, find out if there is available to him a tribunal that will hear his case personally, with some realistic probability of success, and will arrive at a decision expeditiously. These facts can usually be reasonably and quickly ascertained by a direct and open talk with an advocate or a member of the tribunal of the diocese in which the person lives. In almost every instance it is a waste of time to discuss the possibilities of a tribunal solution to a marriage problem with a priest who does not actually work in a tribunal. These are some of the questions that may very legitimately be asked. Precisely what is the basis for annulment or divorce in my case? Exactly how many cases with this basis for nullity or divorce received an affirmative decision in this tribunal in the last calendar year? What was the average time from the day of the first interview until the day the affirmative decision could be acted upon and the person could remarry? If the answer to any of these questions is evasive, vague or on the negative side, this tribunal is not for you.

*

Even with the new procedural rules, the American Norms, half of the tribunals in the United States process either no cases, or one or two cases a year, negative or affirmative. Tragedy breeds tragedy. It can be surely said that many thousands, perhaps hundreds of thousands, in intolerable marriages have no access to a decision, even a negative decision, in the present tribunal system in the United States.

It is impossible to project what a diocese might do in the future because bishops and tribunal personnel as well as policy are subject to change. But the record speaks for itself regarding the unevenness of the "justice" that will be found in various dioceses. For example, the Washington and Newark tribunals grant few annulments. The same is true of the other tribunals in New Jersey. I am sure that along the Atlantic Coast there is not one effective tribunal south of Philadelphia. The Boston tribunal rarely grants as many as fifteen annulments a year. The Rockville Centre tribunal is utterly unable to cope with the number of cases brought before it.

On the other hand, annulments are rarely denied in the Brooklyn tribunal which is now giving hundreds of affirmative decisions annually. The Brooklyn tribunal is one of the more effective tribunals in the United States. It does not seem reasonable, however, that a person's life with spouse and family, that the couple's acceptance in the religious community, their reception of the sacraments—particularly the Holy Eucharist—their burial in the Church, in fact their eternal salvation should depend upon whether they live in Brooklyn or in Boise.

Most of my firsthand tribunal experience has been with the New York tribunal. However, over the past thirty years I have come to know well the work of the many tribunals in the United States for a number of reasons. The New York tribunal was the tribunal of appeal for nine other tribunals. Philadelphia, the tribunal of appeal for New York, was the tribunal of appeal for all of the other tribunals in Pennsylvania. The Newark tribunal, for which New York was the tribunal of appeal, was the tribunal of appeal for all of the other tribunals in New Jersey. Since 1963 I have regularly attended national and regional meetings of the Canon Law Society of America. I was also a member of the Board of Governors of the Society for four years. Since 1964, my articles and talks on marriage have brought me into contact with many priests, some of whom agreed with my views, others of whom did not. My work in 1966 as chairman of the "Committee for the Correlation of the Suggestions of the Bishops of the United States for the Revision of the Code of Canon Law" brought me in contact with two-thirds of the bishops and/or their representatives, usually the presiding judges of their tribunals. My work as the chairman of the committee of the Canon Law Society, which presented to the United States bishops the rules of procedure that eventually became the present American Norms, brought me in contact personally, by mail and by telephone with the priests working in most of the tribunals in the country. For the past several years the Canon Law Society has produced a graph of the number of decisions given annually by most tribunals.

As a result of these experiences I have come to know well, directly or indirectly, the effectiveness or ineffectiveness of the tribunals in the United States. It is my opinion that, since 1938, with the possible exception of the Chicago tribunal, the New York tribunal has been consistently the most effective tribunal in the country. Nearly all of its members were professionally trained lawyers and the few who were not soon became professionals, largely by reason of contact with those who were. While no two tribunal members often agreed on any one issue, we worked together well as a team. Our distinctive individual differences as personalities and our frequently contradictory views generated heated discussions and arguments. From the beginning many of the priests took a great pride in the tribunal. We were proud of our work and worked well as a team. These qualities of the New York tribunal led us to seek out and to apply legitimate creative interpretations of the law and to doggedly and persistently seek out all the available evidence in each case.

By reason of the differences and contradictions in our personalities, our views of the law and our appreciation of the facts, we frequently argued over the merits of a case. In the "hard-core" annulment cases there were always three judges. The "hard-core" cases are those in which the following are the alleged reasons for annulment: 1) physical and psychic impotence, 2) intentions contrary to permanency, fidelity and the right to physical intercourse, 3) force and fear, and 4) lack of due discretion. Each judge had one vote. We sometimes met several times before voting. Many, many times there were two votes in favor of the annulment and one against, or two votes against the annulment and one for it. We processed many borderline cases, cases in which it was difficult to decide whether the annulment should be granted or not. In the course of the years, I found that I often knew beforehand what the decision in these cases would be on the basis of my knowledge of the personalities, views and abilities of the judges. In retrospect, it is clear to me that eternal salvation did not and does not depend on whether the judges in a case were Jones, Smith and Jones, rather than Smith, Jones and Smith. It is even more clear to me that eternal salvation does not depend on whether the judges were Smith, Smith and Smith, rather than Jones, Jones and Jones. While our judgments were honest, independent and reasoned, they were obviously fallible. Another sign of the fallibility of the judges is that in the 1940s and well into the 1950s at least two-thirds of the decisions involving due discretion were negative. In the latter 1950s, the 1960s and even more so in the 1970s, the trend has more than reversed itself. This was due to our becoming more and more aware of the latest findings in psychiatry and psychology. At the present time at least four out of five cases involving due discretion are decided in the affirmative. Again, does eternal salvation depend upon whether you lived in 1940 rather than 1970? In view of what the Church law was at that time, it is questionable that almost any person who tried to obtain an annulment in New York prior to 1938 was admitted to Heaven. And New York was, and is, the green wood. What was happening, what is happening, in the dry?

It should be noted that Cardinal Spellman was proud of the New York tribunal and Cardinal Cooke is now proud of it. Each of them did all in their power to see to it that it was a good tribunal. Moreover, they never moved in on the tribunal. They never tried, I would say they never thought to try, to influence the decisions of any of the members of the tribunal. Not only that, but they welcomed the opportunity to support us enthusiastically when we were creative in our interpretation of the law, trying to effect changes in the law, having difficulties with other tribunals including the tribunals in Rome, or seeking the reversal of a decision made by the pope.

I would emphasize again that New York had an excellent tribunal, and like those in a few other large cities, the tribunal personnel were professionally equipped for their work by reason of formal canonical education and experience. In other cities including some of the larger ones, even though the tribunal personnel may be gifted in other ways they are not educated in Church law. Moreover, they are usually appointed to two or three or more other positions so that it is difficult for most of them to work wholeheartedly in the tribunal without considerable distraction.

More often than not, the other positions they hold are more satisfying than their posts in the tribunal. Frequently they are pastors, directors of vocations, hospital chaplains, etc. With most of us who have been or who are in tribunal work, satisfactory results—insofar as they are possible—are obtained only by an almost relentless concentration on what can easily be or become a distasteful work. I know that my work in the tribunal from 1943 to 1959 was sometimes not of high or even good caliber because I was enthusiastically engrossed in work other than tribunal work. While my heart was with the persons who sought my help in obtaining annulments and divorces, it was not in my tribunal work, where it should have been.

In view of the comparatively few competent judges available in any tribunal and because of the huge number of potential tribunal cases, the one-judge court is a decided improvement in the law. However, the problem of subjectivity remains a problem. If Judge Piccillo, who tends to be liberal, is the judge in your case you may get an affirmative decision. If Judge Dubronsky is the judge, you may get a negative decision. Since Judge Clancy is new in tribunal work and is also the pastor of a large parish, you may get a negative decision because he tends to adhere to the letter of the law and has not yet learned to evaluate properly all of the facts and circumstances in the case. Does your continuing friendship with God depend on whether you come to the tribunal on Monday or Tuesday rather than Wednesday?

Intolerable Marriage and the Tribunal

✻

It is more than a paradox, it is a contradiction that in the tribunal the one area where there is obvious concern and compassion is in the matter of money.

In my latter years in the New York tribunal the annual expenses for the running of the tribunal ran from $130,000 to $140,000. In a good year, we received $17,000 to $20,000 in expenses from our clients. In the Archdiocese of New York the expenses ranged from $25 dollars to a maximum of $225, depending on the nature of the case. Whether a person could pay the expenses or not made no difference in our accepting a case and bringing it to a conclusion as soon as we were able. The deficit of more than $100,000 was made up from archdiocesan funds. We often spent months, sometimes years, trying to ascertain if there were a provable basis for an annulment. Money for expenses was never mentioned until and unless we thought that a case could be presented to the court with a reasonable possibility that it would receive a favorable decision.

Cardinal Spellman frequently asked me to see prominent persons who came to see him about obtaining a tribunal annulment or divorce. Never once did he exercise any kind of pressure nor did he ask whether or not I had been able to help the persons. Very, very infrequently was I able to help them. I might note here that the decisions of the tribunal are just about the only decisions which a bishop—or archbishop—cannot overrule.

One day a prominent good woman, after I had told her I did not think she had grounds for an annulment, asked me if it would do any good if she knew anyone. I asked her whom she knew. She gave me the name of an extremely prominent figure. I told her she could speak to her friend. She asked me what he would do. I said that he would probably speak to Cardinal Spellman and that the Cardinal would speak to me. There was a brief silence. Then both of us smiled. We understood each other and parted in a friendly fashion.

Years ago I thought rotal lawyers charged exorbitant fees. As the years went on I realized that lay ecclesiastical lawyers at the Rota were on a par with civil lawyers in the civil courts in the United States. They were for the greater part good professional men making a living doing work they liked to do and could do well. As a matter of fact, most of the fee, which went to Rome—usually from $1,000 to $1,500—was used for translation of the papers in the case from English into Italian or Latin and for the printing of the papers so that they could be available to all of the members of the Rota.

On numerous occasions, when persons were unable to pay the expenses for the case in Rome, I had no problem in having the case processed without payment of expenses.

While I am most desirous to make it clear that I have never known a case where money was a factor in the obtaining of an annulment, I think it a minor aspect of the tragedy of the tribunal that money is a factor at all. Like so many incidental factors in the tribunal, it is a good or indifferent part of an inherently bad institution.

When a person, directly or indirectly, asks me if an annulment or a divorce can be bought I answer that since Judas sold Christ for thirty pieces of silver, I have no doubt but there have been persons who have tried to buy or sell annulments or divorces. I say "have tried" because a "bought" annulment may be of value in hell but it has no value in Heaven and is certainly a twisted form of Christianity on earth.

Do prominent or rich persons receive more consideration from tribunal personnel than "everyman," the ordinary man, in the complementary sense of the word? My experience tells me that the answer is "No." In fact, I remember a number of instances when tribunal workers were warned, and rightly so, not to discriminate "against" persons because they were rich or prominent. The warning is not without good reason: 1) most priests working in tribunals come from lower middle class families and have a tendency to have more empathy with persons who have backgrounds similar to their own and, 2) fear that granting an annulment to a prominent person might cause scandal.

Psychiatrists, other medical men and other professionals who act as experts in annulment cases are paid a fee. The fee they receive is only a small fraction of what they would receive for spending the same amount of time in the ordinary practice of their profession.

Intolerable Marriage and the Tribunal

These are some interesting facts I observed over the years about expenses in the tribunal: rich persons rarely, if ever, adverted to money as a factor in the case; prominent persons usually accepted negative decisions with unusually good grace; persons of Puerto Rican origin paid the expenses more often and more promptly than other persons; we were often accused in the tribunal offices as well as just about everywhere else of giving negative decisions because persons could not pay for them—which is simply not true.

The price is right given the professional services that are involved in the tribunal procedures. I believe the laws that make the tribunals necessary and govern their procedures are unjust. Further, there is a grave injustice in the unevenness of the way cases are processed in tribunals around the country.

Where there is evident grounds for processing a case, where there is a functioning tribunal and where there is reasonable hope of processing a case under the American Norms, many Catholics will still be interested in submitting their cases. To see inside a working tribunal should be of interest to them and informative for those who have been forced to seek justice elsewhere.

IX

Inside the Tribunal

One of the most compassionate persons I ever met was the late Monsignor John Leo Dolan, one of my predecessors as the presiding judge of the New York marriage tribunal. John's compassion arose out of his sense of the immediate. On one occasion while he was taking a statement from a witness, he asked the question: "Where were you on the evening of June 2?" The witness replied: "I was walking the dog." John immediately asked: "What kind of dog?" The question was ludicrously irrelevant, but John was not. He always had a sense of the person and the mood or lack of mood of the person with whom he was talking. The other person was immediately aware that John instinctively acted on the belief that all men and women are good, or potentially good, and should not be subjected to injustice or unpersonalness. In his own shy way, John was a fearless person. It is my belief that as a person he never became a part of the tribunal system. He may even have thought the system ludicrous, but while working with the tribunal, he always followed the rules. The day before John died, two other priests and I visited him in his bedroom at Saints Peter and Paul Rectory in the Bronx, and John cheerfully worked with us to give decisions in the last three cases on which he was a judge.

The late Monsignor James B. Nash was instinctively the finest judge with whom I ever worked. Jim Nash was not a professionally schooled canon lawyer, yet he was able to eliminate all of the legalistic and unrealistic aspects of a case and reach quickly the heart of the available evidence, sense the unavailable evidence, and within the limits of the law, arrive at a sound conclusion quickly, but never hastily. Given the harsh, unbending fact of the system, his giant kindness and low-key sense of humor were able to soften the blow when he found it necessary, as he often did, to say that a person could not obtain a tribunal annulment or divorce. His personal ability to rise above the system, however, did not really solve the problem of the reason for the unalterable "No" —the law itself.

I have mentioned these priests in particular to emphasize the only possibly right aspect of Church tribunals—the personnel. More often than not, the priests working in tribunals are intelligent and compassionate. Particularly in the larger dioceses, they are often specially trained and skilled in their tasks. The New York archdiocesan tribunal can boast of such men as the late Monsignor Edward Gaffney, the late Monsignor Robert Emmet McCormick and Father Edward R. Daley, a Dominican priest who is one of the present presiding judges of the New York tribunal. All of these priests helped me to be just and kind with everyone, the rich and poor, the men and the women, whether I liked them or not.

There are key personnel, other than priests, in tribunal work. When I became a judge in 1954, I became aware of the dedication of the psychiatrists who worked as experts with the tribunal in cases involving possible lack of due discretion. They worked for a monetary pittance with the thought that they were helping persons and were working as apostles for the Church.

For many years these psychiatrists took it for granted that the priests in the tribunal were fully aware of all of the implications of the law in this most difficult area. Thus, they did not conceive, so far as we knew, of suggesting creative interpretations of the law. This picture changed as the years went on. In 1966, the tribunal priests in New York had their annual meeting and social evening with the psychiatrists, gynecologists and urologists who worked as experts for the tribunal. The discussion phase of the meeting was opened with a brief statement about the contribution the experts could make in suggesting legitimate creative interpretations of the law. It took a few minutes for the experts to realize the import of what was said. Then the floodgates opened. The experts began to talk. Some of them said they had questioned for a long time our strict interpretation of the law. A gynecologist said he had wondered why he was questioned only about his physical examination of a woman. He said easily and surely that a gynecologist could tell more surely whether or not a marriage had been consummated on the basis of the emotional and verbal reactions of the woman to the examination than from the examination itself. One psychiatrist, an excellent expert for the tribunal, felt that the tribunal was an utterly ineffective instrument for the Christian resolution of the problem of the intolerable marriage. He said it would be better if we could find a "just man" to make the decisions and do away with the tribunal. Like so many of the priests, however, these medical experts had worked quietly, devotedly accepting on faith that the Church policy should not be questioned.

Other lay persons, men and women, are also deeply involved in the operation of the tribunal. Presiding judges come and go, as do other priest members of the tribunal. Lay persons, such as the late Mary Mallon, keep the tribunal going year after year and contribute greatly because of their intelligence, their technical abilities and, above all, their kindliness. Mary Mallon was a superb organizer, an exceptionally efficient stenographer and typist and unusually exact in the use of words and language. Without the title, Mary did everything but preside as judge in the New York tribunal from 1944 until she died a short while ago. Mary not only held the tribunal together, she was able to weld it into a reasonable enjoyable human operation. Her courtesy and gentleness with persons seeking relief from the tribunal frequently outdid the efforts of the priests, including myself, in this regard.

In 1961 I was appointed presiding judge of the New York tribunal. It was at this time that I decided that the work of the tribunal could be done well—at least by me—only if I did not become involved in other work. As I became more and more aware of the possibilities of effecting positive changes in the tribunal structure and its procedure, the work became very challenging and most interesting.

Between 1962 and 1968, the lay persons and the other priests in the tribunal working with me did effect positive changes in the New York tribunal. We established a circuit

Inside the Tribunal

court whereby we interviewed persons in Harlem, and persons in the outlying areas of the archdiocese who rarely if ever came near Madison Avenue and Fiftieth Street in New York City. The circuit court taught us that persons were able to talk about the intimacies of their married lives much more easily and more relaxedly in their homes and in parish houses than they were at the tribunal. The circuit court also gave us a more personal contact with parish priests. We introduced priests from religious orders and congregations into the tribunal, as well as parish priests, to work as advocates, defenders of the marriage bond and judges.

We added one layman to our staff of advocates. We met with lay lawyers and judges to try to learn from them how we could improve the efficiency of the tribunal. With great help from the more talented priest members of the tribunal, the psychiatrists and a lay member of our staff, I learned more and more about the possibility that the relative incapacity of a couple in a marriage—their inability to make it with each other, even though each of them may have been as normal as the rest of us—was the basic reason why a genuine marriage never existed or began to exist and then died. With the help of these same persons, I learned that it was most difficult to discern what, if any, guilt, blame or responsibility were present in persons trying to obtain annulments and divorces because their marriages always were or had become intolerable.

I met annually with the presiding judges from the other seven tribunals in New York, as well as the presiding judges of Boston, Newark and Philadelphia. The tribunal of Philadelphia was the court of appeals for the New York tribunal and the New York tribunal was the court of appeals for Boston, Newark and the other tribunals in New York State. We came to know each other more personally and learned from each other. This made it easier for us to work together in cases in which two tribunals were involved. We expanded our staff of medical experts and brought into the tribunal Jewish and Protestant psychiatrists. We made the practice what had been the exception, accepting women as notaries in the tribunal.

It is a paradox that when, in 1968, I became convinced

that the tribunal should be abolished I was transferred from the tribunal with great reluctance on my part. I saw no contradiction in the fact that a judge could apply a law while working for its abolition. In some instances, and for me this was one, the view that a law is not a good law may lead to open thinking about legitimate creative interpretations of the law.

In the last case on which I was working in the tribunal, I was trying with an able and compassionate psychiatrist who was an expert for the tribunal, to obtain a decision, within the law, on the basis of the substantial inability of a couple to complement each other as persons. We were trying to make this breakthrough so that there would be no need to belabor the alleged deficiencies of one person as the cause of the nullity or death of the marriage.

Basic incompatibility is the principal reason couples seek annulment in the Church today. In the law, however, it has never been alleged as grounds for nullity. The principal reason for this may well be that, if basic incompatibility were commonly accepted in practice as the reason for annulment, it would be extremely difficult to discern whether the incompatibility became a fact before or after a marriage. In the former case, we would have an annulment, in the latter case a divorce. This "difficulty" will shake to its very foundations the ancient and time-honored policy of the Church that there is always a clear-cut distinction between an annulment and a divorce. The preservation of present policy, which can be translated "Don't rock the boat," apparently has greater importance in the minds of many churchmen than a consideration of the personnel, the people or the problems engaged in the tribunal.

※

It is well to remember that the persons who appear before Church marriage tribunals, parties to the marriage and witnesses, are a mixture of Catholics and persons of other religious communities, of persons with no religious affiliation or with no religion at all. Some are formally religious but not actually religious. Most are honest, a very few not honest. They are lettered and unlettered, intelligent and unintelligent. They are sometimes verbal to the point of exercising a diarrhea of words. Others are non-verbal to the point of muteness. They are liberal or conservative. They are rigid or relaxed, hostile or friendly.

With almost no exceptions they know little or nothing about the procedural or substantive law of the tribunal and are often burdened with a mass of misinformation about the law. The parties to a case are often confused about the facts; the witnesses are frequently misinformed about the facts. In addition, the parties and the witnesses very frequently find it difficult, impossible, distasteful, hateful, to talk with people they do not know—the advocates and the judges—about the intimate physical and emotional aspects of their own lives as well as the lives of others. Some—considerably more than a few—parties and other witnesses, Catholics and other than Catholics, in annulment cases consider the nature and form of the questioning in the tribunal unduly suspicious, insulting and an unjust invasion of privacy. I agree.

The civil lawyer, as a lawyer, will tend to think of a marriage case as an adversary procedure; that is, a procedure in which one party wants the annulment and the other party does not. This is the presumption in the present law of the Church divorce, or one party is and the other party, for reasons that may be good or bad or simply because of indifference, is uninterested or disinterested. Some are hostile to the Church action, though not to the annulment or the divorce itself. Other persons who are not Catholic—and there are many such involved in cases that come before the tribunal—are simply, and often rightly, hostile to the intrusion of the Church into the privacy of their lives. This same observation is becoming increasingly true of many Catholics.

The diversity and variety of qualities of these persons give rise to further problems in the processing of cases in the light —or perhaps more appropriately, the twilight atmosphere— of the complex and involved nature of the law. Ascertaining the facts—insofar as they are ascertainable—about due discretion, faithfulness, consummation and intentions concerning the right to sexual intercourse is extremely difficult under ideal circumstances. A reticent petitioner, a hostile witness or an impersonal though qualified advocate may simply make communication about the basic alleged reason for the annulment impossible. A judge who is more formal than necessary may further silence a witness who is already reluctant or almost unable to talk about the intimate aspects of his or her life in marriage. A petitioner will sense immediately, and be discouraged and disheartened by this sense, if a priest in the tribunal, qualified and workmanlike though he may be, is basically not enthusiastic about tribunal work or avoids becoming personal with the petitioner. In either direction—in both directions—hostility breeds hostility, impersonalness fosters impersonalness. When there is an allegation that a marriage was not consummated, a man may be unable or unwilling to admit this fact—if it is fact—lest he be suspected, rightly or wrongly, of being impotent.

A father-in-law and a mother-in-law of a man who has, as their daughter tells the story, made her life miserable, may so describe the words and actions of the man, who is possibly no more abnormal than the rest of us, that one wonders why he has not been committed to a mental hospital.

On the other hand, the objectivity of a tribunal can be swayed favorably by the appeal of personality, talent, energy or even by the guilelessness of innocence. One day at the tribunal we were discussing whether or not we were influenced in the processing of a case or in making a decision by the rapport, or lack of it, that existed between ourselves and the petitioner for an annulment or divorce. One priest summed it up well for me by saying, "I find it very difficult to say or do anything displeasing to a young child, an old person or a beautiful woman."

A case comes to mind of a woman who was relaxed, patient, persistent, intelligent, alert and determined to get the annulment. This woman was trying to obtain an annulment on the grounds of bigamy because the man she had married had been previously married and his first wife was still alive. You practically had to have the first wife brought live into the tribunal and put on display before an annulment would be granted on the grounds of bigamy. I made what I thought were unusually good efforts to locate this woman's husband and his former wife. I had no success.

Then, the woman became a one woman tribunal. She

Inside the Tribunal

scoured the nearby states, located both persons and persuaded them to make statements before a priest that made it clear in tribunal law that they had been truly married. The processing of this comparatively simple case took well over a year. The woman was granted an annulment. Her beauty was a comparatively minor factor, but it did make it easy to talk with her and to try to help her. It was her other personal qualities that enabled her to win the case for herself. Very few of our clients were as relaxed, as patient, as persistent, as intelligent, as alert or as determined as this woman was.

I recall another case in which the man, who was the petitioner, was not relaxed and was patient only with great difficulty. His was a formal, a "hard-core" case. He was persistent, intelligent and alert, and he was determined to get the annulment. He was sufficiently well off financially so that he could have his witnesses come to New York to testify. His witnesses were genuinely and honestly co-operative. This latter fact made all the difference in the world in this complex case. If we had had to ask priests in other parts of the country or of other parts of the world to take the testimony of the witnesses, as we often did, we would have been at a distinct disadvantage because these priests would not have known the full history of the case, would not have had rapport with the petitioner and might have found the witnesses unwilling to testify.

There is scarcely need to explain that often enough a rare combination of circumstances was necessary before an affirmative decision could be given. Any one of the following could effectively lead to a negative decision: the refusal of the other party to testify or to release psychiatric evidence; the unwillingness of witnesses to co-operate; the necessity of obtaining testimony through another tribunal; a lack of intelligence and alertness in the parties to the marriage or in the witnesses; the inability of the parties or the witnesses to state clearly what they knew about the case; a lack of rapport between the priest taking the testimony and the person giving the testimony; a lack of persistence on the part of the petitioner to obtain an annulment. Many fine persons who came to the tribunal, and they may have been as good or better than the petitioners in the two cases described above, simply did not have any or all of the elements described above. Does a full moon mean a negative decision? Does a quarter moon mean an affirmative decision? Were all of these persons alienated from God? To put it mildly, I doubt it very, very much. Within the tribunal, however, a rare combination of tribunal personnel, tribunal policy, the legal complexity of the problem, the personality of those with the problem, and the rapport of all the people involved will determine the resolution of a petition to live in peace with a second spouse. I do not believe that salvation depends on the happy concurrence of such circumstances.

*

A number of actual cases will exemplify how the tribunal utterly fails to meet the real issues and to solve the real problems of the people who come seeking a pastoral solution to one of the major problems of their lives.

CASE ONE

A lovely Catholic young woman—lovely in a moral and religious way as well as lovely in an emotional and physical way—had known a religious Protestant man for many years. They were in love with each other. If they had not actually planned marriage, they were thinking of marriage when the man went overseas in service and remained overseas for several years. The man was lonely, but he saw no value in casual intercourse with women nor in living outside of marriage with a woman. He married a native girl he liked and who liked him. They were scarcely married when they both realized that this was nothing more than an arrangement of convenience. They both had made a mistake. They were alien to each other, they could not be persons with each other, they could not tolerate each other in marriage. The girl disappeared. The man returned home and resumed his interrupted romance, and they wanted to be married in the Catholic Church. There was obviously no provable case for a tribunal annulment. Since the entire family of the girl, including the girl herself, were members of a religion in which baptism did not exist, there appeared to be hope that there could be a tribunal divorce because the girl had obviously never been baptized. Neither the girl nor her parents could be located. It was decided that, according to tribunal standards, it had not been proven that the girl had not been baptized. The Catholic girl became very bitter. I remember this well because I was the object of her bitterness, but I was working in accordance with tribunal standards. The Protestant man obtained a civil divorce or annulment. He and the Catholic girl were married in the Protestant church and she now attends the Protestant church with him.

CASE TWO

A Catholic man was given an affirmative decision by a tribunal in Europe. In accordance with the law the defender of the marriage bond had to ask the tribunal of appeal to reverse the decision of the first tribunal. Before this second decision was given, the man moved to the United States. While he remained in Europe he considered himself, and was considered by many Catholics, as outside the Church because he was divorced. He was not considered a candidate for marriage in spite of the fact that the first tribunal had given an affirmative decision.

Some years after his arrival in this country he learned that the tribunal of appeal had given a negative decision. He appealed to the Rota. After almost endless further questioning by the Rota, questioning that obtained no more information than had been obtained by the first tribunal, the Rota gave an affirmative decision. From the time the man was first interviewed by the first tribunal until the Rota gave an affirmative decision, ten years had passed. The man never met any member of the second tribunal. He never met any one of the three rotal judges who gave the final decision. In the course of the ten years, he married outside the Church. During the course of the ten years, he was amazed and puzzled and angry—and probably still is—at the anonymity, the impersonalness of the tribunal and the obvious fallibility of the judges of the tribunal.

CASE THREE

A woman trying to obtain an annulment had her first interview in New York in 1951. She received an affirmative decision in New York in 1955. Philadelphia, the first court of appeals, reversed this decision in 1956. The next step would have been to send the case to the Rota. The woman became discouraged, dropped the case and married outside the Church. In 1967 she asked that her case be sent to the Rota. This was done. Here is a classic example of what happens when a case becomes anonymous and impersonal. I was in Rome around 1968 or 1969 and asked how the case was progressing. As I have mentioned before, the rotal judges were, in person, gracious and human. The same was true of the secretarial staff. I spoke with one of the secretaries. He checked the case and told me with chagrin that it had been misfiled and no one had looked at it since it arrived in Rome. In early 1971, the woman's advocate in Rome, who was, and is, a gentleman and a good canon lawyer, informed her that an affirmative decision had been given. It was only after several months of constant urging that the New York tribunal was informed officially of the decision.

Finally, the woman was married in Church in the summer of 1971, twenty years after the first petition for annulment. If the woman had come to the tribunal in 1965 the case might have been finished in two years. If she had come to the tribunal in 1971, it might have been finished in less than a year. In this last instance, the time period may not seem unreasonable to some persons. The reason for the annulment in this case was that for years prior to the marriage the man had been very seriously mentally ill. This was a medical judgment. In my opinion, the priests in tribunals are not capable of making medical judgments. At best, they can say that these judgments seem to be reasonable or unreasonable. Would it not have been much better if, in 1951, a priest had simply said to the woman: "Since you surely and honestly know that you and this man are unable to live together in marriage, it is important that you obtain a divorce and then decide thoughtfully whether or not you desire to marry again. Neither your marriage, nor your divorce nor a marriage in the future will affect your status in the Church. You are a good Catholic and will continue to be one."

CASE FOUR

A Catholic man came to the tribunal in 1941 seeking an ecclesiastical divorce for the reason that his marriage had not been physically consummated. In 1944, after all of the available evidence had been obtained, Cardinal Spellman, on the recommendation of the priest in the tribunal who had worked on the case, sent the case to the Congregation of the Sacraments in Rome with the recommendation that the divorce be granted by the pope. On two occasions the Congregation requested further information. A negative decision was given in 1946. The man married a Catholic woman outside the Church. He and his second wife observed faithfully all of the laws of the Church. Because of Church law, however, they did not receive Holy Communion. They raised their children to be good and positive Catholics. In 1967, the man, without saying anything to his wife or anyone else, came to the tribunal and asked me if anything could be done to have the decision reversed. I looked at the written record of the case. It was about two inches thick. In view of the length of time that had passed, and in view of the fact that the Congregation of the Sacraments had made two further inquiries after reviewing the evidence in the case, I told the man that I doubted anyone could help him. Rome had spoken. The case was closed. After the man left the office, however, I carefully read the evidence in the case and was convinced that the decision should have been affirmative rather than negative. I spoke with an older priest in the tribunal who was familiar with the case. He told me that this man was the most honest person who had ever come into the office. I prepared a letter for the Cardinal in charge of the Sacred Congregation of the Sacraments, a letter to be signed by Cardinal Spellman. In this letter I said that this other priest and I were in agreement that the negative decision had been a mistake and that Cardinal Spellman agreed with us. I also asked that the case be reviewed and explained briefly why I thought the decision should be reversed. Cardinal Spellman read the letter carefully—as he always did—asked me a few questions and signed the letter. In the latter part of 1968 or the early part of 1969, the then Archbishop Cooke received word from Rome that the case had been reviewed and the negative decision had been reversed. The couple were married in Church and received Holy Communion for the first time in almost twenty-five years.

Three of the four cases described here eventually had happy endings. It is well to remember that the vast majority of cases do not end happily—even with the comparatively liberal changes effected by the American Norms. Less than one out of ten cases presented to the New York tribunal are settled favorably. Another way to see the great disparity between the potential number of cases and the actual functioning of tribunals is to note the fact that in 1972 there were more civil divorces among Catholics in the diocese of Brooklyn than there were tribunal decisions in all of the United States.

These facts reveal how the Church and the tribunals are utterly failing to serve the faithful in marriage cases.

Following the publication of my critical article in *America*, in 1968, and following my 1972 appearance on NBC's "Today Show," I was deluged with hundreds of letters in which persons told me they had been unable to obtain tribunal annulments or divorces, and asked if I could help them to be able to receive Holy Communion. At that time I was able to help only a few. Are all or any of these persons to be deprived of union with God in heaven—and on earth—because they married a second time without the benefit of a tribunal divorce or annulment? My response to that question is an emphatic "No." And it is absurd to expect human beings to wait years for the Church to condescend to say whether or not they are to be accepted back in the fold.

X

Reasons for Divorce and Annulment in Church Law

Perhaps the most distressing aspect of Church law regarding divorce and annulment is that the substantive law itself—the grounds put forward by the Church for granting divorces or for declaring annulments—has little or nothing to do with the petitioners' reasons for seeking a divorce or annulment. The result is that often the tribunal procedure is so artificial as to be absurd. At best it is a game of looking for the "loophole" that will allow escape from the problem without facing up to the real issue—that a marriage has died. At worst it becomes a pharisaical adherence to legal formalities with little or no relationship to the facts or circumstances that brought on the death of the marriage.

To exemplify the point, let us first look at the provisions of the law and then offer some observations with regard to the practice of the tribunals.

I. REASONS FOR DISSOLUTION OF MARRIAGE (DIVORCE) IN CHURCH LAW

1. THE LAW

A. *Lack of Physical Consummation.*

A sacramental marriage, that is, a marriage between two baptized persons, may be dissolved if it has not been physically consummated.

1. By the pope for a good reason.
2. By the solemn religious profession of one of the parties.

B. *Absense of Baptism in One or Both Parties.*

1. PAULINE PRIVILEGE—When there is a valid marriage between two unbaptized persons and one becomes baptized, he obtains the right to remarry if the unbaptized party re-

fuses to cohabit peacefully. The dissolution is brought about by the remarriage of the baptized person. The Pauline Privilege is exercised under the supervision of the local bishop.

2. PETRINE PRIVILEGE—Any marriage in which at least one party is unbaptized may be dissolved by the pope.

2. Observations About the Legal Practice

A. *Physical Consummation.*

I remember a case in which Cardinal Spellman, in accordance with the law, was to give an affirmative or negative recommendation before a decision would be given in Rome by the pope as to whether or not a marriage had been physically consummated. If the pope decided in the affirmative, he would be granting a divorce. The priest responsible for processing the case drew up a thorough draft of a recommendation for the Cardinal. The Cardinal questioned the recommendation and sent it to me in view of my responsibility for the overall work of the tribunal. I wrote a contrary recommendation and sent both recommendations to the Cardinal. He then asked me to have a third priest, a man who had worked in the office many years before I, write a recommendation. This latter priest wrote a recommendation agreeing with the first recommendation. The Cardinal chose one of the three and sent it to the Sacred Congregation of the Sacraments in Rome. A total of at least five priests and bishops, and a cardinal, reviewed in whole or in part the evidence in the case, and the cardinal in charge of the case then asked the pope to give an affirmative decision on the basis of the recommendation of Cardinal Spellman. This the Holy Father did, and the petitioner was declared free to marry.

The only person who actually talked with the parties to this marriage was the priest who wrote the first recommendation. Neither I nor the priest who wrote the third recommendation nor Cardinal Spellman ever met the couple. No one involved with the case in Rome met the couple. Cardinal Spellman did not read the evidence in the case. I doubt that the Cardinal who asked the Holy Father to give an affirmative decision read the evidence in the case. I do not think it would be humanly possible for the Holy Father to read any, or certainly no more than a few, of the thousands of such cases presented to him each year for decision.

This case illustrates for me the utter lack of realism and the almost pharisaical concern for material adherence to the letter of the law in decisions in cases of this kind—cases in which the basis for the divorce, not an annulment, is the lack of physical consummation of the marriage. Other than the parties to the marriage, the only person who may have had an opportunity to make a healthy personal subjective decision—and every decision in marriage cases is subjective and should be personal—was the priest who personally talked with and took the testimony of the couple in the marriage. In this particular case, the persons who actually made the decision were the doctors who physically examined the woman and were in substantial agreement that she had not had physical intercourse with any man. As an aside, imagine the distaste—to use a mild word—a woman must feel when a doctor, sometimes four or five doctors, examine her genital organs for reasons which have nothing to do with medical care. Besides, the indignity of the procedure is aggravated by the fact that it is totally unnecessary except for the satisfaction of a grossly materialistic and formalistic, even pharisaic, interpretation of the law. The examination has no moral, spiritual or sacramental value even to the social and sacramental dimension of marriage—and even less value in determining the personal dimension where real marriages are made or destroyed.

It is my opinion that no priest, bishop or pope, is able to make a sure judgment that a marriage has not been physically consummated. At best, in some instances, they may be able to affirm the knowledgeable judgment of a doctor or doctors who, at times, may be able to make a sure judgment. Even doctors are rarely able to make such a sure physical judgment. In most instances, only married couples can—and even they often enough are unable to be certain—make a sure judgment as to whether or not they had real intercourse according to the legal definition. Certainly only they can say whether or not they physically made love as a sign of their marital affection for each other, and the physical evidence is meaningless, unless all the Church is interested in is to judge spiritual reality on the basis of an unbroken hymen.

If the Church in the person of her ministers is to be involved at all in the annulling or dissolving of marriages because of the fact that a couple did or did not physically make love—and I do not think that she should be—she can only, at best and at most, accept the word of the couple as to whether or not they lovingly consummated their marriage.

According to Church law, only the pope can dissolve a marriage that has not been physically consummated. If the pope has the power to make this decision he must do it by divine inspiration since he does not know the parties to the marriage or the facts in the case. If the pope is divinely inspired to dissolve the marriage between Joseph Smith and Mary Jones, there is no need for the lengthy, time-consuming, tedious, distasteful work which now precedes his decision. But the pope is not divinely inspired to make such decisions. The pope knows this. He should not be making these decisions.

B. *Pauline and Petrine Privilege*

In the teaching of the Catholic Church a marriage between baptized persons, whether or not either or both are Catholics, is a sacrament. The marriage is "signed" by God in a special way.

The teaching of the Catholic Church, however, that she may dissolve a marriage in which either or both parties are not baptized, raises a practical problem. Since at least two-thirds of the persons in the world are not Christian, whether they like it or not, and whether they know it or not, their marriages can be dissolved by the Catholic Church. Since most of these persons never heard of the Church and very, very few of them would be in any way affected by the Church laws, they could not care less what the Church teaches. However, there is a basic issue at stake here. There is nothing in the Scripture to justify this teaching. When Paul said that a newly baptized Christian could divorce his unbaptized wife and marry again, he said that the divorce could take place because of intolerable religious differences between the couple. He did not say that the simple fact of one person being baptized and the other person not being baptized was reason for a divorce. He did say that an intolerable marriage of this kind could be terminated by divorce and that the Christian could marry a second time. Marriages become intolerable for reasons other than religious differences. These reasons, because they are deeply personal and intensely human, have just as much, sometimes more, value as religious differences. It is well to note, too, that in the history of the Church the Pauline practice was rarely if ever used in the first thousand years of the history of the Church.

In view of all of the foregoing I find it most unrealistic for the Church to teach that a true marriage can be terminated on the basis of the fact that one or both of the parties have not been baptized. Moreover, if a marriage can be terminated because of intolerable religious differences, and I think this can be done, it can also be terminated because of other substantial intolerable differences. In other words, if the Church permits divorce in one kind of intolerable marriage, she should permit divorce in every kind of intolerable marriage.

Finally, in all of my years of experience in tribunal work, every use of the Pauline Privilege, without exception, was and is used after a marriage has become intolerable for reasons having nothing to do with baptism or religion. The Church today is using the skeletal provisions of the Pauline Privilege and has extended even these skeletal provisions to the Petrine Privilege so that she is granting divorces in marriages in which only one party is not baptized. In fact, the Church is permitting divorce for reasons quite distinct and different from the reasons clearly set down by Paul. She is acknowledging that a true marriage is dead, that a couple cannot live together, and she is giving as the reason for the divorce the unrelated fact that one or both of the parties have not been baptized.

Obviously, the reasons for the divorce are twofold: the first marriage was or became intolerable, and the petitioner either wants to remarry in the Church or has already remarried civilly and wants to be admitted to the sacraments. In either case, the Pauline or Petrine Privilege is used as an escape from the intolerable marriage to open the way for a valid second marriage. But the Pauline or Petrine Privilege does not meet the problem of the intolerable marriage head-on. In the case of a Catholic couple whose marriage may be just as intolerable and their need to remarry, or having been remarried, their need to be restored to the sacraments is just as demanding, or even more demanding, there is no escape, no recourse in the law. Yet the reason of both petitioners is exactly the same. The first has a legal "loophole"; the second does not.

II. REASONS FOR ANNULMENTS OF MARRIAGE IN CHURCH LAW

1. The Law

A. *Cases Involving Invalidating (Diriment) Impediments.*

1. Age—16 years for a man; 14 years for a woman.

2. Impotence—The antecedent and perpetual incapacity of a man or a woman to perform acts which of their nature are apt for the generation of children. These acts consist of the penetration and emission of true semen within the vagina.

3. Bigamy—The previous and still-existing marriage of one party.

4. Holy Orders—If man is a subdeacon, deacon or priest.

5. Solemn Religious Vows.

6. Disparity of Worship—between an unbaptized person and one who is baptized in the Catholic Church or has been converted to the Catholic Church.

7. Abduction—The violent abduction and retention of a person for the purpose of marriage.

8. Crime—This arises because of:
A. adultery with a promise of or an attempt at marriage, or
B. adultery with the murderer of a lawful partner.

9. Consanguinity—Blood relationship that exists between persons in the direct line of descent or between those who descend from a common ancestor in the collateral line (to the third degree; i.e., second cousins).

10. AFFINITY—Relationship that exists between one party to a valid marriage and the blood relatives of the other (to the second degree; i.e., first cousins).

11. PUBLIC PROPRIETY—Relationship that exists between one party and the blood relatives of a party with whom he has contracted an invalid marriage or with whom he has lived in public or notorious concubinage (to the second degree; i.e., first cousins).

12. SPIRITUAL RELATIONSHIPS—Relationship between a baptized person and the person who administered baptism, between a baptized person and his intended spouse.

13. LEGAL RELATIONSHIP—When a legal relationship, e.g., by reason of adoption, is an impediment in the civil law it is also an impediment in Church law.

B. *Cases Involving External Manifestations of Consent.*

1. When there is a basic defect in a marriage in which a proxy or interpreter is involved.

2. When the person assisting at the marriage is not properly recognized by the bishop of the diocese in which the marriage takes place. The general rule is that a priest approved by the bishop assists at a marriage in which at least one party is Catholic. In a mixed marriage, with the permission of the bishop, the assisting official may be a minister of another religion, a rabbi or a civil official. A marriage that is invalid because of a substantial defect in this area is said to be null and void because of defect or lack of canonical form.

C. *Cases Involving Insufficiency of Consent.*

Insufficiency of consent may be related to the intellect, the will and/or the emotions.

1. IGNORANCE—The parties must at least be conscious that marriage is a permanent society of a man and a woman for the procreation of children.

2. THE INTENTION NOT TO COHABIT or to enter the common life with the other party.

3. LACK OF CONSCIOUSNESS at the time of marriage; e.g., because of drugs or alcohol.

4. ERROR about the other party to the marriage or a substantial quality of the other party.

5. SIMULATION OF CONSENT:

A. *Total simulation*—The mental exclusion of marriage itself despite the words and actions signifying consent.

B. *Partial simulation*—The positive mental exclusion of faithfulness or indissolubility, or the positive intention to qualify the right to conjugal acts forever and at all reasonable times.

6. CONDITIONAL CONSENT—This is similar to simulation of consent.

7. FORCE AND FEAR—When marriage is contracted under pressure of grave fear, engendered by unjust external force, so that a person is compelled to choose marriage. Reverential fear, i.e., fear of parents, will invalidate a marriage if it bears the above characteristics.

8. LACK OF DUE DISCRETION—This is the lack of that maturity of judgment necessary and sufficient to understand, choose, undertake and fulfill the responsibilities of marriage, whether this be a transitory or habitual disturbance, whether it be progressive or static. In present tribunal practice, most annulments are granted because of lack of due discretion. In general, this basis includes any insufficiency of consent as described above that is not contained in numbers 1 through 7.

2. OBSERVATIONS ABOUT THE LEGAL PRACTICES

Today, the impediments of disparity of worship and spiritual relationship are pure legalisms. They are in no way related to the nature of marriage and should simply be eliminated as impediments. Holy Orders and Solemn Religious Vows should not be considered as impediments inasmuch as a person, in the present law, wishing to forego the practice of Holy Orders and/or the formal religious life should simply be dispensed and considered free to marry. The other impediments, if they are to be impediments, should be the concern of the civil law. I do offer these comments on physical impotency as a reason for tribunal annulment. The obtaining of evidence in these cases is often a torture for one or both parties. Physical impotency should not be a reason for an annulment. In the vast majority of marriages, physical sexual intercourse plays a most important part. However, there can be a marriage, a union of the persons, of a man and a woman, without such intercourse; e.g., a marriage between elderly couples, a marriage in which an impotent paraplegic is a party. Whether a man or a woman is impotent is their business and is often a problem for them. It is not the business of religion or the Church, nor is it the province of the Church to resolve the problem.

We will content ourselves in the remainder of this chapter with a few comments on the grounds for annulment that are most common in Church tribunals: A) defect or lack of canonical form, B) simulation of consent, C) force and fear, and D) lack of due discretion.

A. *Defect of Canonical Form*

While it must have happened more than fifteen or twenty years ago, the incident is very vivid in my memory. A distinguished looking and personable woman came to the tribunal. She was a Protestant who had been married to a Catholic for a number of years and they had had several children. She had just found out that her husband had quickly and easily obtained a tribunal annulment of their marriage in the Catholic Church because they had not been married by a priest. She was puzzled and pained. And so was I. The incongruity is almost incomprehensible. Some people try for years to obtain an annulment or divorce because of serious, long-lasting incompatibility, and here was a case in which a husband walked away from a marriage easily and quickly on a technicality that had nothing whatsoever to do with the intrinsic quality or value of the marriage.

According to Church law at the time this incident took place, a marriage in which at least one party was baptized in the Catholic Church was not recognized as a true marriage by the Church unless an approved Catholic priest assisted at the marriage. It is worthy of note that this rule prevailed although the Church at the same time taught and teaches that the parties actually marry each other and if they are both Christian they confer the Sacrament of Matrimony upon each other. The presence of the priest is basically as a witness representing the Christian community.

The law that was in force at that time concerning a marriage between a person who is a Catholic and a person who is other than Catholic has changed considerably since the above described incident took place. Now, a couple is able to arrange for a marriage in a Catholic, Protestant or other church, or in a synagogue, with a Protestant minister or rabbi formally assisting at the marriage rather than a priest. I recently made arrangements with a rabbi so that I might assist at a marriage in the synagogue of a Catholic man and a Jewish girl. I agreed that in the ceremony there would be no reference to the Christian teaching about the Trinity. In another instance, I arranged for the marriage of a Lutheran girl and a Catholic man in the Episcopalian Church with a Protestant minister assisting. The marriage was to take place in a small town in a diocese other than New York. At the time of the arrangements, which were made with the approval of the local bishop, we did not know the name of the minister who would assist or the denomination to which he belonged. In many places the marriage may take place in a home, on a lawn, in a hotel, etc. The decision as to whether or not a marriage may take place outside of a place of worship is at the discretion of the local bishop. Arrangements may also be made with Church approval for a marriage before a civil official. These have been some of the most heartening changes in recent times in the law of the Church on marriage. The changes in the law place the emphasis where it should be, on the fact that the couple marry each other. They are not married by anyone else, including God. However, the approval by the bishop of the official assisting at the marriage is still necessary for the validity of the marriage in the Church.

I hope that in the not too distant future no Church approval will be needed relative to the place of the marriage or the capacity of the person who assists at the marriage. Then it would be very clear that the couple are marrying each other, as has always been the fact, and it would be presumed that they are responsibly working out between themselves the fulfillment of their religious responsibilities. There would be no question of the marriage being annulled or dissolved because of an element not substantially related to the nature of marriage.

B. *Simulation of Consent*

The ideal beginning of any marriage embodies the live dimension of the personal, thoughtful, willful intention on the part of each person to share marital affection with one another until death without calculated reservation, particularly in the areas of mutual faithfulness and fruitfulness. Hopefully, in God's mysterious personal providence this marriage will continue indissolubly until death. The first fruit of marriage is the growing of each party in their giving their persons to each other. In most marriages, especially among younger couples, a second fruit of marriage is a child or children and the bittersweet experience of helping the child or children form themselves into healthy and wholesome adults.

It is difficult to be mathematical or diagramatic, it is difficult to formalize, to confine within a verbal, legal framework, these living, dynamic dimensions of marriage. So it is that, over the centuries, in an effort to help couples obtain ecclesiastical annulments, canon lawyers have ingeniously and, one might say, creatively interpreted the letter of Church law in the areas of faithfulness, indissolubility, and love-making. I purposely said that "one might say" that these interpretations are creative because, in my opinion, they are, for the greater part, ultimately—and initially—unreal in that they try to put lines around the unlineable and they are, frequently enough, not related to the true reason why the marriage never existed or existed and later died.

There have been cases where a man was known to have been making love to his mistress until very shortly before the marriage and resumed making love with her shortly thereafter, but the woman he married was unable to obtain an annulment because she was unable to produce clear legal evidence that, despite his conduct before and after the marriage, he definitely excluded fidelity when he verbalized his marriage vows. Then there was a man who practiced the evil art of deflowering virgins. It was only after his marriage that he had intercourse with his wife for the first time. Even though the marriage, if there ever was a marriage, never truly became alive and deteriorated rapidly, it was simply impossible, in this case, for the girl to prove that her husband did not intend to be faithful to her when he married her.

There have been cases where even though a man had been publicly known to have lived with several women before his marriage and left his wife shortly after their marriage to live with another woman, the wife was unable to prove clearly in legal form that he had excluded permanency at the time of the marriage ceremony.

Possibly the most unrealistic basis for an annulment of a marriage in Church law is an intention by either person at the time of the marriage ceremony to make any reservation of the giving of the right to physical sexual intercourse. Just a few years ago, I recall the New York tribunal confirming the affirmative decision of the Rochester tribunal, declaring a marriage null because the man had an intention at the time of the marriage to practice birth control for the first few years of the marriage. Affirmative decisions along the same lines are not uncommon in many tribunals.

It is my impression that in this day and age there are very few couples who exchange the right to have physical sexual intercourse without substantial reservations. A good advocate could attack the validity of almost any marriage on this basis. If this particular basis for an annulment is real, there are very few genuine marriages, Christian or otherwise, in the United States. It is worthy of note that a man could obtain an annulment on this basis if his wife insisted on using the rhythm method of birth control contrary to his will.

C. *Force and Fear*

Force and fear as grounds for annulment are deceptive in terminology and very narrow in meaning. In ecclesiastical legal jurisprudence these words are rigidly restricted to specific types of force and fear. It must be clearly proven that the force is unjust. It must be clearly proven that the fear is so overwhelming that there is no alternative to a clearly unwanted marriage. While I easily appreciate the fact that force and fear may make a genuine marriage impossible,

I am also aware of facts which, to my mind, strip this reason for an annulment of any substantial value. There are some marriages in which either or both parties were unjustly forced to marry, or married because of a realistic substantial fear, and then, because of human unpredictability, made their marriage good, healthy and productive of joy and healthy children. Moreover, there is no provision in Church law for the annulment of a marriage in which a man or woman was forced to marry unwisely to get away from an intolerable situation in his or her home. There is no provision for the annulment of a marriage entered into unwisely because of loneliness, a desire for sexual gratification, a yearning for a continuing relationship with a person of the opposite sex, the fear that he or she may not have another opportunity to marry. There is no provision for the annulment of a marriage when a couple feel compelled to marry because they have been going together for years and feel it impossible to tell their families and friends that they have come to know that they never were in love with each other or have fallen out of love.

In our society, are not these and other reasons such as the premarital pregnancy as compelling on the couple as the "shotgun" wedding of the hill country or the feudal military alliance of old? If force and fear is a "real" reason for annulment, why isn't "force and fear" understood realistically, as it exists today in our society?

D. *Lack of Due Discretion*

The alleged reason for annulment in most dead marriages is the lack of due discretion in either or both parties at the time of the marriage.

The phrase "lack of due discretion" is deceptive. On Willis Avenue in the Bronx we would say, "He is crazy," or "One of his wheels is missing," or "He is a nut." If we were trying to be polite, we might say, "He's different from the rest of the family." The person who is judged to be lacking in due discretion is stigmatized as unable to contract marriage, as insane. Only a few years ago the word "insane" was customarily used in tribunal terminology. This is wrong. It is not Christian. It is not human.

Lack of due discretion is the most common grounds for annulment in tribunal practice today. The reason is simple enough. There is no provision in the law, not even recognition by the law, that marriages which meet all other legal requirements for validity may become intolerable. If that should happen, Catholics have no escape but to try to prove the marriage was null and void from the beginning because one party to the marriage was insane prior to the wedding.

More will be said about due discretion in the following chapter. Here it is worthy of note that in every case discussed in this chapter the real reason for seeking a divorce or an annulment of a first marriage is that the first union dissolved, died, ceased to exist as a viable relationship and one or both of the parties is or wants to be remarried. The law of the Church completely ignores this fact as a "real" problem to be dealt with directly and solved equitably.

For the unbaptized who never belonged to the Church and who make up the majority of people in the world, for those members of the Church who married outside the Church and who make up a sizable minority of Catholic marriages, for those whose marriage was not consummated, the Church provides relief from the intolerable marriage with the right to remarry. For her faithful sons and daughters who married exactly according to her rule, there is only the possibility of the rare annulment, usually on the grounds that one party was insane at the time the marriage was contracted. If a person should remarry without the ecclesiastical annulment, the Church has but one answer—EXPULSION—expulsion from the active life in the Church, expulsion from the Eucharist, expulsion from Catholic burial.

XI

Basic Incompatibility Is the Only Reason for Dissolution

One Sunday morning, as I was on my way for a walk in Central Park before saying Mass at Holy Name Church at Amsterdam Avenue and Ninety-sixth Street, I saw from a distance a man coming toward me whose disheveled hair and beard appeared even dirtier than his disheveled clothes. My first and spontaneous reaction was a pious ejaculation, "May Jesus Christ help him." As we drew abreast I saw that the dishevelment was real and externally total. My second thought was a more probing evaluation, "Jesus Christ he could be."

I think of this story as an example of how difficult—often impossible—it is to make a sure judgment on the basis of external appearances. I think of how dangerous it is to make a negative or damaging statement about a person unless it is surely true and made with good reason. It is for this reason that, to my mind, the most unchristian aspect of the present jurisprudence in the tribunal is that a marriage may be declared null because one or both parties is declared to have been so emotionally or mentally disturbed at the time of the marriage that he or they were incapable of marriage. In ecclesiastical legal language it is stated that the person lacked "due discretion." When one woman heard this phrase for the first time she said, "I never met him." In real life, only very rarely, if ever, is a marriage unreal because of one or more deficiencies in only one of the parties. If and when this does happen, one would tend to suspect the discretion of the second party if he did not have a sense of the deficiency of the first before the marriage.

The present law has forced the tribunal advocate seeking a solution to an intolerable, but consummated, marriage of Catholics, to claim grounds for annulment on the basis of some condition predating the wedding. For sincere Catholics who have gone through the Church in contracting their first marriage, there is little possibility of lack of form, force and fear, presence of diriment impediments, etc., on which to base petition for annulment. The majority seek to prove that one party was incapable of contracting marriage from the very beginning. It has to be shown that one party was so lacking in judgment, in maturity or in emotional or mental health that he or she was incapable of effecting the marriage union. This completely ignores the fact that two relatively normal persons could have incompatible qualities or that two rather abnormal persons who might fit the description of "lacking in due discretion" could have an "insanely" happy marriage.

There are schizophrenics who, whether we like it or not and whether we consider it scientific or not, are happily married to each other or at least would be less happy if they were not married to each other. The psychopath is an anguishing problem to himself and to those who love him. At the same time there are marriages in which the other party might find life more intolerable if deprived of her psychopathic mate. And yet the majority of annulments in Church tribunals are based on the fact that one party lacked due discretion because of schizophrenia, homosexuality, psychopathy, sociopathy, anxiety neurosis and other clinical diagnoses. In the Brooklyn tribunal the technical, mechanical and clinical psychiatric techniques are so well developed that hundreds of annulments are granted annually on this basis. I recall one competent and compassionate psychiatrist remark that annulments were being declared by diagnostic epithet.

My question is: Where on earth is Christ in the presence of this ecclesiastical finalistic judgment about the incapacity of a person to marry? To my mind, he is not there. His Church should not be there. The Church should not be using this cruel method so that persons may be free to marry again within the Church.

Only recently, I met a woman who was tortured because her husband obtained an ecclesiastical annulment on the grounds that she lacked due discretion at the time of the marriage. As I listened to the facts in the case, I had the same sense I had had in at least a hundred other cases. It was clear to me that the man, in this instance, had been more lacking in discretion than the woman at the time of the marriage. The premarital and postmarital conduct of the man had been shocking. The woman had not mentioned this conduct in the tribunal because she considered it a private matter.

It occurred to me, as again had happened many times before, that the failure of the marriage, if there had initially been a marriage, was not due to any unusual or abnormal emotional or mental disturbance in either party but to the simple and tragic fact that they, each of them or both of them, were unable or unwilling to have marital affection for each other. In this instance, the woman felt, and rightly so, that the Church had stigmatized her, in a sense crucified her, by labeling her with a clinical diagnosis. She asked me if she should try to have the decision reversed. Since the man had already remarried in the Church and since an attempt at a reversal of the decision would have to be made in Rome, I suggested that she let the decision stand. At least, it left her free to marry in the Church, and taking the case to Rome would be a nightmare. The decision, when it did come, would necessarily be anonymous and impersonal. She would not meet personally any of the personnel of the tribunal in Rome, not even her own advocate or attorney.

As I look back over the years, I recall a number of cases in which something very similar occurred. Once a party seeks an annulment on the basis of the lack of the discretion of the other party all action on the part of the tribunal zeroes in on this point. There is little or no advertence to the possibility of lack of due discretion in the other party. I distinctly recall a case in which it was blatantly clear that the conduct of the man alleged to lack due discretion was obviously the result, at least in part, of the clear inability of the woman to be a person with him. The woman was granted an annulment. I recall even more distinctly another case—in which I had spoken with both parties—in which the inability of a particular man to accept and receive his wife as a person was the reason why she acted in a bizarre fashion after the marriage. She was all woman. The man, the petitioner, was unable to be emotionally and psychologically a person with her. He was granted an annulment.

If priests were subjected to the same investigation as the parties in such marriage cases, many would be found lacking. If canonical due discretion had to be proved for ordination to the priesthood, or if the validity of Holy Orders could be challenged after ordination, we might lose more priests than we are already losing because they are marrying and/or seeking a more satisfying life outside of the priesthood. Lest some readers feel neglected, I will extend myself to say that if proof of due discretion were required for attendance at the Eucharistic celebration, we might lose a goodly number of our congregations.

The intended humor of the above paragraph is meant to suggest that "discretion" is a variable that has different meanings for different people. It cannot be squared or circled or wrapped up in a psychiatric diagnosis. On a recent occasion when a few persons were discussing the marriage of Mamie and Willie, the consensus was that they could not understand how Mamie could continue to live with Willie since Willie was obviously crazy. One man expressed surprise to the point of astonishment and exclaimed that he thought Mamie was crazy. A woman closed the discussion by saying: "Some can live with it, some can't." My own conclusion was that Mamie and Willie may both have been crazy and neither could care less that the other was utterly lacking in discretion. In their own crazy way they were happy, they were making it together. While they might be perplexed to hear that they had marital affection for each other, they would have been delighted to know that other persons realized they were in love.

Some married couples simply enjoy their enjoyable marriages. Other married couples are able to tolerate their tolerable marriages. Still other married couples are unable to tolerate their intolerable marriages. They cannot or will not make the marriage work. At least one of them cannot tolerate the other.

Each marriage is a unique union of two unique persons. The tribunal tries to give a scientific answer to the question why particular marriages were initially intolerable by mathe-

Basic Incompatibility Is the Only Reason

matically analyzing the personality of either or both parties. It is not possible to do this. It is like trying to give the reasons why some persons are gloomy on sunny days, why some persons are sunny on gloomy days and why still other persons are sunny on sunny days and gloomy on gloomy days. It is like trying to explain why some persons like to walk in a driving rain.

You cannot make an analysis of the personality of one person in a marriage or of each person separately and arrive at the true reason why the marriage was never a true marriage or why it lived for a time and then died. The answer to these questions is found in the interaction of the two persons. More often than not each person could have married a hundred other persons and entered a true and lasting marriage. These two persons should not have married each other. They did not, in fact, enter a lasting marriage. They were mutually and basically incompatible as persons from the beginning or they became incompatible after marriage and the marriage died.

At a meeting with the psychiatric experts of the tribunal the discussion turned on the meaning of "due discretion." As each doctor gave a different specific medical explanation of what he would consider "lack of due discretion" sufficient for an annulment, it became apparent to me that the only reason a marriage never was a marriage or was a marriage and died was that this particular man could not make it as a person with the person of the particular woman he married. They could not or would not complement each other. They could not grow as persons in their marriage. Each might have been a person basically fit for marriage, but they did not fit each other as persons. They frustrated each other. They hurt each other. They diminished each other. They sickened each other and the marriage died. Sometimes one or both of them died with it.

The Church will never cover the tracks of its often energetic, but always pathetic, effort to solve the problem of the intolerable marriage by reverting to annulment on the grounds of a pre-existing lack of due discretion. It is a subterfuge. The facts are: 1) that the existing intolerable marriage is the problem, 2) that personal incompatibility which is existing, observable, defineable and irremediable is the cause of the problem, and 3) that the only solution is to face the facts as they exist.

The position adopted here is not an isolated opinion, a voice crying in the wilderness. The need for change in the basic approach to the intolerable marriage is the concern of lay persons, pastors, priests, scholars and lawyers. It must become the serious concern of the entire Church.

XII

A Search for Change

There is to me little indication that substantial, thorough, lasting reform will come from the top. My experiences in Rome as a consultor to the Pontifical Commission for the Revision of the Code of Canon Law, lead me to think the contrary. For example, I found no one even listening to my opinion that it was simply unrealistic—I might add impossible—for the Holy Father to reasonably dissolve or annul a marriage. An equally stunned silence greeted my statement that if the Holy Father insisted upon giving decisions affecting the marital status of two persons, he had a responsibility to talk with the persons and to give the reasons for his decisions.

Even minor revisions are looked upon with suspicion as the following experience concerning a minority opinion indicates. When there are three judges sitting on a case it happens often enough that two will vote in the negative and one in the affirmative. In the present law when a decision is written and presented to the parties it is sometimes a collegiate sentence; that is, three judges sign the one decision. For example, if I had voted in the affirmative, I would sign the negative decision that had been given by the other two judges and written by one of them or by myself! When I first became a judge, in 1954, I was perplexed and puzzled, and at least slightly disturbed at the thought that I was signing an important document which I was convinced was a misstatement of fact and sometimes of law.

However, this was one of a number of instances where I became a victim of the tribunal, and for many years I continued to do what, in these instances, I knew was wrong. I was taking part in somewhat of a star chamber proceeding, which was most misleading to the parties when they were faced with a very legal-looking document signed by all of three judges in the case. I do not recall one instance where the parties suspected that there frequently had been a strong dissenting opinion.

When our committee of eleven consultors in Rome considered this point I made a strong plea for the publication of a dissenting opinion when there was one. At first, my suggestion fell on deaf ears. However, after a long and tedious argument we agreed, with a majority of one or two, that we would suggest that in the new law the dissenting opinion would be mentioned and that the parties could read it if they wished to do so. This was one of the few times when those of us who were interested in trying to make radical changes in the law met with any success.

On other levels, however, efforts to effect change are being made. There are already many organized outlets through which laity, religious and priests may forcefully make the pope and the bishops aware of what they think should be the status of divorced Catholics who have remarried or desire to remarry. The day is gone, I believe, when laity, religious and priests will implement laws that are obviously not good laws and are not accompanied by reasonable explanation.

On August 30, 1970, I asked Father Frank Bonnike, the president of the National Federation of Priests' Councils, to offer the following resolution to the Federation for action:

> Whereas the Eucharist is the source and center of unity in the Church and millions of members of the Church in second marriages are deprived of the Eucharist; and
>
> Whereas the recent changes in tribunal procedure (the American Norms), helpful as they are, are not adequate to cope with the numbers of persons who seek Church annulments and divorces in their marriages; and
>
> Whereas as many as half of the dioceses in the United States cannot provide priests who are trained and experienced to adequately staff tribunals; and
>
> Whereas lay persons, men and women, who alone have lived through the experience of marriage, are presently excluded from being judges in tribunals; and
>
> Whereas many of the present matrimonial laws of the

Church are based on premises devoid of a consideration of the dynamic quality of the human person and of the married couple; and

Whereas reliable judgment about the existence or non-existence of a marriage can be made only by the parties to a marriage and by persons in direct contact with these parties; and

Whereas some tribunals, and many individual priests and lay persons, are now functioning outside of the present law of the Church,

BE IT RESOLVED

1. That the Canon Law Society of America be urgently requested to seek legislation whereby lay persons, men and women, may be judges in matrimonial cases, and whereby all marriage cases, without exception, may be resolved on the diocesan or local level and,

2. That the Catholic Theological Society of America be urgently requested to probe the possibility of Catholics in second marriages being fully welcomed at the Eucharistic celebration even if it cannot be determined with certitude whether or not their prior marriages were true marriages, and

3. That the Bishops of the United States be urgently requested to encourage the efforts of these two Societies and to give full consideration to the implementation of their recommendations.

The resolutions were adopted unanimously by the executive board of the Federation at its August 1970 meeting. The Canon Law Society of America and the Catholic Theological Society, in October 1970 and in June 1971, respectively, established committees to consider the implementation of the first two resolutions.

*

The Committee of the Catholic Theological Society, whose chairman was Father John R. Connery, S.J., submitted its findings at the annual meeting of the Society in September 1972. The Committee statement, which was printed in the

October 7, 1972, issue of *America*, contains the following noteworthy comments:

"[There must be a] constant proclamation of the meaning of marriage in Christ and its indissolubility, preparation for permanent marriage and support for existing marriages.... There are Catholics (in second marriages) whose marital status in the eyes of God does not correspond to their legal status. Also, there are unions, e.g., where children are involved, where it may be morally wrong to terminate the relationship. Many will not understand how it will be possible for them to sustain this relationship without marital union. We do not think these people should be excluded from the Sacraments or participation in the life of the Church. If a couple decides after appropriate consultation, reflection and prayer that they are worthy to receive the Sacraments, their judgment should be respected."

※

Father Lawrence G. Wrenn, the presiding judge of the tribunal of the Archdiocese of Hartford, was the chairman of the Committee of the Canon Law Society of America. With the approval of the general membership of the Society, he has gone beyond the letter of the resolution as originally written and has conducted a study that points to the resolution of marriage cases by methods other than the tribunal. The results have been published in a book entitled, *Divorce and Remarriage in the Catholic Church*, edited by Lawrence G. Wrenn (New York: Newman Press, 1973). The contributors to the study, aside from canon lawyers, include sociologists, psychologists, historians of Church law, anthropologists and theologians as well as scholars of other science. The reason for this is that most canon lawyers today are aware that good law cannot be formulated on a theoretical or ideal level without assessing the facts of the lives and the circumstances of the persons who will be affected by the law.

The Canon Law Society of America has 1,400 members, including some members from Canada. (Canada has its own Canadian Canon Law Society which works in close co-operation with the Canon Law Society of America, as does the

Canon Law Society of Great Britain.) Most of the members of the Society are priests who work in tribunals and/or chancery offices. The membership also includes professors of Church law and moral theology in seminaries, universities and colleges. There are several lay women who are members and a couple of dozen sisters; that is, women religious. The dozen or so laymen who are members include Stephen Kuttner and John T. Noonan, Jr., two of the foremost historians of Church law in the world. Noonan is the author of *Power to Dissolve—Lawyers and Marriages in the Courts of the Roman Curia*. It is an excellent scholarly work which from an historical viewpoint deals with the basic questions I have raised here.

As is clear from the overall contents of this book, my own thinking has evolved considerably beyond the resolutions presented in 1970 to the National Federation of Priests' Councils. In the spring of 1971 I was invited to present my views—the views I have set forth here—to the New York Senate of Priests. The Senate is a group of fifty priests elected by all of the priests of the Archdiocese of New York. The Senate is a consultative body to Cardinal Cooke who meets monthly with its executive board. While no vote was taken, there was only one strongly dissenting voice, and three or four mild dissenters in the discussion following the talk. Since most of the members of the Senate are parish priests, part of whose work is to refer persons with marriage problems to the tribunal, it was heartening to have a half dozen or more of the senators come to me after the meeting to express agreement with the views I had presented.

I have urged the National Federation of Priests Councils to encourage the presentation of these views at meetings of senates, councils and associations of priests whether they are voted upon or not. Over the past few years I have had the opportunity to present my views to local chapters of the National Association of the Laity, interfaith gatherings, Jewish and Protestant congregations as well as a number of Catholic groups including a chapter of the Judaean Society whose members are divorced Catholic women intent upon practicing their faith.

※

Many times in history, substantial changes in Church law have come about slowly. At other times, changes came about overnight in what may be described as a revolution in one form or another. In 1970, when I wrote the resolution for the National Federation of Catholic Priests, I thought the tribunal was here to stay for some years and that if the resolution beame effective in law, more cases would be processed more expeditiously so long as the tribunal was a functioning, if not a flourishing, institution.

Certainly it would be preferable to have all cases solved on a local level. Decisions by tribunals in the United States other than the one selected by one or both parties to a marriage would be excluded. Decisions by the Rota, the Signatura, any judge or judges in Rome, including the Holy Father, would be excluded. The elimination of decision-making in Rome would clear up considerably the anonymity and unpersonalness that necessarily accompany Roman decisions and any decision made by a person or persons who had not been in direct and open contact with the parties to a marriage. It would also cut down considerably the amount of time consumed in the processing of cases. It would virtually eliminate the large expenditure of money in tribunal work. Above all, it would release the hundreds of the many competent priests in Rome for work that is Christian and relevant to the spiritual growth of persons and communities.

But all of these changes, even if they could be put into effect tomorrow, would only prolong the agonizing death of the tribunal system. The tribunal is so substantially out of touch with the reality of the Church and the world today, that accidental changes in procedure and personnel, or even further major changes in ecclesiastical jurisprudence, some of which I think highly questionable, will not make the tribunal good or real.

The tribunal is dying. This would appear to be contradicted by the fact that there are many more affirmative than negative decisions, both in terms of numbers and in terms of the number of cases being heard, than ever before in history. Notwithstanding these facts, for a number of reasons I say the tribunal is dying. Most of the priests dedicated to tribunal work in the few comparatively efficient tribunals in the United States are close to or over forty-five years of age. Many of them probably find it impossible, as I did during many years of service in the tribunal, to see anything substantially unreal about the system while working within it.

The tribunal is a fascinating game from within, but the Church should not play games with persons' spiritual and religious lives. I question seriously that the few young priests, good and talented as they may be, who will accept assignment to the tribunal will have the dedication men had in the tribunal twenty years ago. The men at that time were dedicated to the tribunal or, because of the temper of the Church, were willingly subject to an obedience which sometimes commanded a devotion to do unwarranted and unreasonable work. This concept of obedience is dying out in all areas of the Church among many laity, religious, priests and bishops. More and more priests, especially young priests, but some older ones too, are ignoring tribunals and helping persons responsibly obtain a civil divorce, remarry before a minister, a civil official or rabbi, and to continue to participate in the Eucharist. Many lay persons, without the helping hands of priests, are responsibly and maturely acting in this way on their own. For these reasons, and for the even more substantial reasons—the internal reasons—set down elsewhere in this book, the tribunal is dying. For a very large number of Catholics, lay and clergy, the tribunal is dead.

XIII

The Good Conscience Solution

Since efforts to change the laws and procedures governing the tribunal processing of marriage cases have failed to date, many responsible persons—bishops, canon lawyers, pastors, priests—have attempted to by-pass the law and the traditional tribunal procedure. As of June 1972, Bishop Robert E. Tracy of Baton Rouge, Louisiana, publicly permitted the so-called "Good Conscience Solution" in some cases in which couples in second marriages had been unable to obtain a tribunal annulment or divorce in their prior marriages. His position was that a couple are considered to be in good conscience if they are convinced that they are truly married, and if they are convinced that the prior marriage of either or both were not true marriages. Since their convictions were not provable in tribunal procedure, they were considered to be in good faith as to their convictions. They were permitted to participate actively in the Eucharistic celebration and to receive Holy Communion, even if these convictions were not based on fact. This solution, or one very similar to it, was first used on a wide scale in the Archdiocese of Chicago as early as 1945. A form of Good Conscience Solution has been used publicly in Boise, Idaho, and in Portland, Oregon.

On August 17, 1972, John Cardinal Krol, the president of the National Conference of Catholic Bishops, announced that the Holy See had made it clear that procedures contrary to current Church discipline were not to be introduced. This statement clearly implied a ban on the Good Conscience Solution and was so understood and accepted by Bishop Tracy. However, the Good Conscience Solution did receive widespread publicity, and it is still applied privately in a variety of forms by many priests and lay persons. This, of course, has its advantages and disadvantages.

In his letter to all of the Catholics of the diocese of Baton

Rouge, Bishop Tracy explained his reasons for originally allowing the Good Conscience Solution: "The Church has a pastoral responsibility of healing and forgiveness, following the example of Christ, without giving the impression that she condones divorce and remarriage or that she had given up any of her firm beliefs in the sanctity and life-long character of the marriage vows and married life."

Bishop Tracy's statement was brave and strong. It was to me a healthy sign that Bishop Tracy and at least two other bishops had publicly initiated this practice. Moreover, I am reasonably sure that there were other bishops who agreed with Bishop Tracy. Some of these latter bishops, while they did not make their views known as publicly and as clearly as Bishop Tracy, have permitted without criticism the priests of their dioceses—and in some instances their tribunals—to put the same practice into effect. In dioceses in which the bishops did not even silently allow the practice, or who had forbidden the practice, there are many priests who were—and are—putting it into effect. If a person searches diligently, it will not be difficult for him to find a priest who will permit the Good Conscience Solution.

I disagree with Bishop Tracy when he says that the Church should not give the impression that she condones divorce and remarriage. There are many, many instances where the Church should encourage persons to obtain divorces. When a marriage is dead, that is, when it has become irreparably intolerable for one or both parties, divorce is the only answer and a person has the right to remarry. The Church should often encourage such a person to divorce and to remarry.

Every dead marriage has elements of tragedy. Brooding over tragedy only aggravates the tragedy. For millions of persons a second marriage is frequently a necessary human need. Often this need is accompanied by the equally important need to be welcomed fully and openly into a religious community. It is a tragedy of major proportions that this truth has been acknowledged by all major Christian communities and by the Jewish community but has not been recognized by the Roman Catholic Church. The intolerability of a first marriage may make the right to marry a second time a more pressing need. An obvious instance of this would be where a man had found the beginnings of marital affection in the initial stages of his first marriage and is starving for the affection in a sure abiding form. Another instance would be where a man or a woman is left with one or more young children, where the children need a new father or a new mother.

Every person has an inalienable right to marry. It is for the person, man or woman, to decide whether or not he chooses to exercise this right. No one in the Church or the state can take this right from him. When a person has suffered through the anguish of a marriage that is now dead, the right to marry remains. The fact that a marriage is dead does not kill the right to marry even though, in this instance, it is a second marriage. As a matter of fact, when a person has desired and intended to marry, and has in fact married once, he has manifested a personal choice for married life beyond the selection of one particular person as mate.

There are persons who because of the make-up of their personalities, or because of the bitterness engendered by their first marriages, or because of their own sense of heroic idealism are able to forego their right to remarry. These persons are few. Only God knows which of them are practicing heroic virtue. Some divorced persons would benefit from psychiatric care so that the bitterness would be removed from their lives. With psychiatric help they could come to know themselves better. They could appreciate better the reasons for the death of the first marriage and how they could knowledgeably seek out the persons who would be for them the right partners in marriage. Without expressly stating it, the Good Conscience Solution at least recognizes the need for some victims of a broken first marriage to continue living in a second marriage.

In the Baton Rouge procedure the persons desiring to avail themselves of the Good Conscience Solution were referred by their parish priest to the chancellor of the diocese for a decision as to whether or not they might receive Holy Communion because of their sure and honest conviction that their present marriage was the first true marriage for each of them. Except in the most extraordinary case, the chancellor

The Good Conscience Solution

accepted the word of the parties and told the couple that they might receive Holy Communion. This makes sense because he was simply putting a seal of Church approval on the right of the parties to participate actively in the Eucharist. He was not making a decision or a judgment in the legal sense of these words. It is my experience that few chancellors are qualified to make this decision; that is, to decide judgmentally whether or not the convictions of the couple are sure and honest. Chancellors are rarely equipped by reason of education or experience, and by reason of their manifold other works, to evaluate the facts in the case, especially the psychological and emotional factors—even when these facts are presented clearly by the person or persons involved.

I saw the Good Conscience Solution, especially when publicly approved by a bishop of a diocese, as a great step forward. However, it does in some cases now, and will in more cases in the future, cause confusion and a genuine or neurotic sense of guilt. There is in this solution something of the same false image and the same false certitude that are the most dangerous attributes of the tribunal. I have already mentioned that ordinarily a chancellor is not equipped to give the required decision. Neither the parish priest nor the chancellor normally is as well equipped to make the required decision as a professional, personal, experienced psychologist or a married person. However, I do not think any of these persons are capable of actually making an effective decision that the convictions of the couple have been made in good conscience. At best, they can agree with the convictions of the couple. It would be a most rare instance when they would be able to say that the couple was lying.

To my mind, the most serious defect in the Good Conscience Solution is that couples are rarely able to say with sureness, not to mention certainty, whether and why their first marriages never truly existed or whether they existed and died. The inability of most couples to make this "either-or" decision with sureness will, in many instances, later generate a true or neurotic guilt if they realize they were not as convinced as they thought they were, and if they realize that the decision of the chancellor or anyone from the bishop on down was not truly a decision and added nothing to their convictions or to their right—or absence of right—to go to Holy Communion.

The Good Conscience Solution is a much better solution than the tribunal solution. However, it is confusing and frequently enough will be an erroneous solution. The confusion and the errors can be cleared up only if, once a marriage is obviously dead, whether it was ever a true marriage or not, the Church acknowledges that the couple are rightfully free to divorce and marry again.

A great weakness in the Baton Rouge procedure was that permission to receive Holy Communion was given only to couples who had lived together for some years and had evidenced that they were living in a stable, healthy union. I cannot understand why the same permission is not given to couples who have not yet married a second time but state that they intend to enter a loving, faithful, lifelong union when they marry. Their conviction that their forthcoming marriage will be a true marriage, their only marriage, may well be as sure and secure, if not more so, than the same conviction on the part of a couple who have been married a number of years. Once the Good Conscience Solution is used, it should be used all the way without unnecessary caution or precautions.

Finally, it may well have been a good thing that the Church went underground into the catacombs during the first three centuries of its existence. However, the underground churches of today are undermining the openness that should be a marked characteristic of the Church in today's open society. There is, to me, a sign of the underground-church approach in the Good Conscience Solution. It would be much better and much more reassuring to couples in second marriages if the Church would say clearly that their union or intended union is a true, good and healthy marriage. This is most important if couples in second marriages are to help their children grow into wholesome adults, and if in entering and living in their second marriages they are to try to be fruitfully and faithfully and lastingly in love.

It is essential for the Church to acknowledge dead marriages as non-existent, to acknowledge openly and joyfully the right of persons who have anguished through dead marriages to renew themselves in second marriages. It is essential that they be, not condescendingly admitted or tolerantly received, but welcomed by the Church with open arms and open hearts as they enter into and live through their second marriages.

XIV

Second Marriage and Full Membership

It is reasonable to acknowledge the right of a person to be an atheist, an agnostic or a worshipper of the obelisk in Central Park. It is equally reasonable to acknowledge the right of a person to be a member of any religious community be it Jewish, Catholic, Protestant, be it any community a person considers religious. This basic right is limited only by the condition that the actions flowing from a person's religious beliefs do not substantially affect adversely the health and welfare of the family, the local or world community of persons.

It is quite as unreasonable to say that there is no basic difference between religions as it is to say that one religion is as good as another. A devout Jew will necessarily deny that Christ is the Son of God. A devout Moslem will, at best, acknowledge that Christ is a prophet second to Mohammed. A devout Catholic sees the Old Testament as the Word of God and the Jews as a Chosen People of God. He will say, too, that the New Testament, the story of Jesus Christ, the Son of God—and the story of the Holy Spirit—is the completion of the Word of God contained in the Old Testament. In these latter beliefs, a Catholic would be flatly contradicting basic beliefs of Judaism and Mohammedanism. These are but a few examples of the fact that religious beliefs, especially the beliefs of the religions of ancient lineage, differ markedly and, at least in their major doctrinal tenets, contradict one another. When a person is trying to practice his religion faithfully, his actions will reflect his religious beliefs. A strict Orthodox Jew may find intolerable the idea of marrying a practicing Catholic. A Moslem man would find it intolerable to have his children—certainly his male children—baptized and brought up as Christians. A devout Catholic would find it impossible to become a Jew in order to marry a Jew and vice versa. The members of the Orthodox Church will consider the possibility of the pope being first among equals; that is, first among the Christian bishops of the world. The Orthodox Church will simply not consider reunion with the Roman Catholics if the abolition of divorce in the Orthodox Church is one of the conditions of a proposed reunion.

In a faith and action sense, the core belief of a Catholic is his belief in the Eucharist, his belief that the Living Body of Jesus Christ is actually and in fact present in the Eucharist, in Holy Communion, under the appearances of bread and wine. A Catholic believes that the life, suffering, death and resurrection of Jesus Christ, God and Son of God the Father, is renewed in the Eucharist. His other beliefs flow from this: that since Christ is God as well as man, Mary, his Mother, is the Mother of God; that the Holy Spirit, who is also God and is the personified mutual love of the Father and Son, comes to us in a real sense in the sacraments—visible signs of God's presence—which lead us to and complete our participation in and reception of the Eucharist. The celebration of the Eucharist carries with it both a deep community action and an intense personal awareness of oneness with Christ.

Catholics are concerned to be in good standing in the Catholic Church, to be acknowledged as active members of the Church, so that they may live in union with their Catholic community and when they die be buried in a grave consecrated or blessed by the Church. Concern for Catholic burial is one of the ways a Catholic shows his desire to be on good terms with God. If a Catholic knows the true meaning of mortal sin—substantial alienation from God—he rightfully and reasonably tries to avoid mortal sin. He may, and often does, become confused and not infrequently neurotic—if not psychotic—if he necessarily equates mortal sin with seeing an XXX movie, or the precise inches or millimeters of a man's—or woman's—body he may touch, or even a rigid view about compulsory attendance at Mass every Sunday.

We are not presently concerned with aberrations be they personal, institutional-based, or both. We are concerned with the substantial intention and will and desire of Catholics that they be not alienated personally from God or the Church, a

Community of God's People. We are concerned with the intention, desire and will of Catholics to be united personally with God and with his Church. Catholics fulfill this intention, desire and will when they have a sure knowledge, a sure sense that they are free to responsibly receive Holy Communion, when they know that they are welcomed at the Eucharist as individual persons and as members of the Catholic family. This is the only substantial relevant question for a Catholic from the moment he is aware he is a Catholic until the moment of death: Am I responsibly free to receive Holy Communion, to participate in the Eucharistic celebration?

In many areas, because her sense of responsibility to the individual person and her awareness of her need to be the Compassion of Christ, the Church refrains from responding to this question in the negative except in the most rare of instances and only when she is certain that the answer must be negative. For example, many Catholics, clerics and lay persons, are racist. There are as many racist riots, disorders and tragedies in Catholic centers as in other centers of the country. If a person is consciously and knowingly a racist he is committing a grave disorder, he is alienating himself from God. Yet only in the most extreme cases will the Church withhold Holy Communion from a person who appears to be a racist. Her attitude in action is: Only God knows all the circumstances. It is rarely just or merciful for the Church to judge negatively with finality.

Another example. Given the richness of the United States and allowing for the need of her many responsibilities to her own citizens, it is obviously good for the Church to foster foreign aid to the more than two-thirds of the world which is hungry and sick and never heard of Jesus Christ. The Church does this in an official and formal way and tries to do it in a practical way; e.g., through Catholic Relief Services and the Campaign for Human Development. Many individual Catholics, government officials and other citizens, are strongly opposed to foreign aid. This is a civic and moral disorder, yet I do not know of one instance in which the Church has denied Holy Communion to a person opposed to foreign aid. I do not question this because only God knows the motives and

Second Marriage and Full Membership

circumstances that prompt a person to act in a way that may seem to me or to someone else to be immoral.

There are other examples. The Church welcomes fully at the Eucharistic community celebration Catholics who appear to be opposed in principle to labor unions, Catholics who oppose low and middle income housing in other than slum areas, Catholics—legislators and citizens—who relentlessly oppose liberal immigration laws. Again, the Church compassionately presumes that the person is acting in good conscience.

The above examples describe situations in which the dignity and the God-given equality of millions of individual persons, men and women, is adversely affected and in which hate, bitterness, indifference, hostility as well as verbal and physical violence become embedded in persons and families in local communities and in the world community. Again, it is very rare that Catholics are denied Holy Communion when they participate in these situations.

When a couple has separated with finality after an intolerable marriage one or more of the following occur to each party: loneliness, bitterness, relief, a sense of failure, an openness to extra-marital physical sexual activity, rejection by family and friends, bewilderment and/or injury to children, a desire for companionship with members of the other sex. Mistakes and evidence of poor judgment which led to the tragedy may be discernible. In most instances, it is very difficult, often impossible, even for the couple or for a psychiatrist, to assess blame, guilt or responsibility, if there were any. One thing that is clear, in most marriages, is that the couple entered the marriage with as good intentions and desires as they were able to muster concerning fruitfulness, lastingness and faithfulness. A second thing that is clear is that they did not make it.

At this point, the Church steps in and says: "You are still married. Unless you are able to obtain a tribunal annulment or a divorce you may not marry again. If you do marry again without an ecclesiastical divorce or annulment, you will be barred from Holy Communion." Where is Christ in this scene? He is not there. In some places, there is no realistic possibility of trying to obtain an ecclesiastical annulment or divorce. When this is possible it is often accompanied, especially in cases involving due discretion, by a belittlement of at least one of the parties. Since the tribunal laws attempt to diagram the living dynamics of the human person and the dynamics of a couple's marital affection, there is considerable likelihood that the decision will be wrong because the very reasons or bases for annulment and divorce in the Church are not rooted in reality.

Against the background of these facts, there are two other facts which are wholesome, human, healthy and holy. They are the right of persons, including Catholics, to live in marriage and the right of Catholics to receive Holy Communion. These are basic human rights. Given the human make-up of persons, those who have suffered and anguished their way through an intolerable marriage have a right to remarry. Most divorced persons have a need to remarry. All Catholics have a right and a need to receive Holy Communion. Aside from the area of sex and marriage, the Church very rarely denies this second right. In the areas of human behavior where millions are being killed, scarred, wounded and deprived by military, racial and economic injustices, the Church does not deny any sacrament or service to those Catholics who may be largely responsible for much of the wounding and the suffering of multitudes. Why is the attempt to find in a second marriage a lasting love and the solace of the sacraments the great insufferable sin for Catholics?

In the aftermath of an intolerable marriage, each person has a chance to find himself, to regain his dignity, to make another person happy, to bring peace and harmony into the lives of his children, to become once again an open, healthy member of the community. The Church denies Holy Communion to these persons if they do not obtain an ecclesiastical annulment or divorce. This is wrong. It is not Christian. It is not human.

It is not at all clear that for at least the first thousand years of her existence the Catholic Church of the West denied Holy Communion on anything like a universal scale to persons who divorced and remarried. Because of the basically negative approach to sex and marriage of some of the Fa-

Second Marriage and Full Membership

thers, such as St. Ambrose and St. Augustine, the Church has in fact frowned upon sex and looked upon marriage as a necessary human weakness. Less than a thousand years ago, the Church became totally committed in discipline and in law to the contractual elements of marriage and to the indissolubility of every physically consummated marriage between baptized persons. This total commitment is presently unrealistic. Substantial radical changes are clearly due. The first change on the part of the Church should be in its attitude toward sex and marriage. There must be an activated awareness that full sexual union—mind, will, body, emotions—which generates lasting affection and helps spouses complement each other as persons, is natural, good and holy. There is need for a reawakening of Catholics to the fact that those who have suffered an intolerable first marriage and who wish to remarry should have a better, more human, more Christian solution to their problem than anything offered them today either over the counter or under the counter.

*

I offer an alternative to the tribunal solution and the Good Conscience Solution to the problem of the intolerable marriage. I describe the alternative as the "Welcome Home" solution. It is my conviction that once a marriage becomes irrevocably intolerable and existentially dead, each party to the marriage, regardless of his religion, has a clear right to divorce, to marry a second time and to be accepted in the religious community of his choice. For the Catholic, this means principally that he will be fully welcomed at the Eucharistic celebration, that he may receive Holy Communion on an equal basis with other Catholics. It means, too, that without exception he will have the same rights as other Catholics in all activities of the Church; e.g., to be the president of the Parish Council. He will be at home in the Church. Moreover, while a person has a responsibility to seek guidance and counsel in such a serious matter, he ultimately makes the decision himself. It is my conviction that the Church community may refuse active participation in the Eucharist only in the most unusual and extraordinary cases where a person has clearly shown a blatant disregard for the basic values of marriage.

This Welcome Home solution is the only human and Christian solution for our time in history. It is not contrary to the words or mind of Christ as manifested in the New Testament. The witness of history is not contrary to the Welcome Home solution.

From the very beginning, the Eastern Christian Church has allowed for divorce and remarriage for a variety of reasons because couples were unable to live in peace. The Orthodox Church from the beginning has admitted exceptions other than the one mentioned by Paul. The Roman Catholic Church has and is granting divorces where there is no religious element truly involved because persons are intolerable to each other, because they are not able to live together in peace. In the context of our time in history, the Church can and should allow for further exceptions so that Catholics who are divorced and remarried may participate actively and joyfully in the Eucharistic celebration. If a divorced Catholic knows that the death of his first marriage was due to willful wrong actions on his part, he should do penance for this fault. But, unless he hears a genuine Welcome Home from the Church community, he is not a free member of the Church nor can he joyfully participate in the Eucharistic celebration. And there is no celebration unless it is joyful.

The Catholic parties to a second marriage should not be forced to live in a limbo of a civil marriage. The Church cannot marry couples; it merely witnesses the marriages of those members within the Catholic community. The Church cannot divorce couples, but it can and should witness the fact that the marriages of some if its members do die. It is not difficult to discern.

Catholics who wish to remarry after the death of an intolerable and irremediable marriage should ordinarily have their marriages blessed publicly by the Church and should be actively welcomed with open arms and warm heart in the central act of Catholic worship, the celebration of the Eucharist. With the protective love of the Eucharistic and a genuinely Christian community, they may well find a greater happiness and joy and holiness than they could possibly have anticipated in their first marriage.

Epilogue

When this book was first published in 1973, its purpose was fourfold: (1) to advocate the abolition of all Catholic Church marriage tribunals; (2) to vindicate the right of persons to divorce themselves if their marriages are irretrievably broken down and existentially dead; (3) to vindicate the right of divorced Catholics and Catholics marrying divorced persons to marry publicly in the Church; (4) to vindicate the right of these Catholics to full membership in the Church and particularly their right to open participation in the Eucharist.

In 1969, approximately 600 annulments were granted by Catholic Church tribunals in the United States. In 1975, there may have been as many as 16,000 tribunal annulments. This dramatic improvement in tribunal performance is due to relaxed procedural norms and liberalized grounds for annulment. However, the improvement is relatively insignificant when we consider the sociologically established fact that there are well over 5,000,000 divorced Catholics in the United States and their number is increasing. No improvement in the tribunal can come close to resolving the problem of these millions of persons afflicted by the tragedy of divorce. Moreover, as is demonstrated in the book, tribunals are neither realistic nor Christian.

More and more lay persons, with and without the aid of priests, are making use of the "Good Conscience Solution" described in the book and are devising good conscience solutions of their own. These good conscience solutions are not the answer to the problem. They are essentially private or secret solutions. The Catholic Church is a public community. If persons are to be welcome in the Church, they must be welcomed publicly.

The good conscience solution fails to face the central issue that the Catholic Church is a Church of law and that Church law follows Church teaching. The good conscience solution is defeatist in its appraisal of the possibility of change in Church teaching. The impediments to change are not greater than those that had to be overcome to achieve the modern ecumenical reconciliation. Nor are they any more formidable than the obstructions which, only fifteen years ago, blocked the emerging role of religious women and men and of lay persons, particularly women. From the viewpoint of lay persons particularly, the right of a divorced person to remarry is as sound as the right of a priest, now effectively recognized by the Church, to leave the active ministry to enter marriage. It is the conviction of many persons, myself included, that theological and Scriptural and historical findings as well as sociological factors are such at the present time that they urgently call for the vindication of the latter right now. We seek the vindication of this right in law. We seek provision for Christian divorce. Moral justice requires a positive statement in law of legitimacy regarding divorce and remarriage, as well as the concomitant right to participation in the celebration of the Eucharist.

I hope that the Bishops of the United States and the Pope will respect the personal dignity and safeguard the marriages of the citizens of the world as well as the citizens of the Church.

May the Catholic Church abolish marriage tribunals, may the Church avoid all circumventions of the present unjust and unrealistic law relating to annulment and dissolution of marriages. May She reevaluate and change the authoritative interpretation of Her teaching concerning the indissolubility of marriage.

May the revised authoritative teaching give rise to a law which will recognize both the right of persons in irreparably broken marriages to divorce and remarry and the rights of Catholics in these latter marriages to participate freely and joyfully in the Eucharist. May the law resulting from the revised teaching set forth clearly the circumstances under which a first marriage may cease to exist. May this law specifically acknowledge that the right to remarry of a person whose marriage has died is as surely sacred as the right of a person to marry the first time.

May the Church establish in Her law a Marriage Counseling Commission which would be available to couples whose marriages show signs of breaking up. The Commission would initially counsel these couples to try to freely and responsibly live up to their commitments to a permanent marriage. In the event that a couple find this commitment impossible of fulfillment, the Commission would acknowledge their right to divorce in a Christian way and would help them, if they so desire, to enter upon a healthy second marriage.

Such a law would be responsive to one of the great human needs of our time. It would be a sign that the Catholic Church is where the people are.

Now is the time for more individuals and groups, especially the laity, to speak with and write to our Bishops on these issues. If the authoritative interpretation of the teaching of the Church and the law of the Church are to be changed, the Bishops must hear the loud and clear voices of divorced Catholics, Catholics married to or desiring to marry divorced persons, Divorced Catholics Groups, Parish Councils, Catholic Physicians' Guilds, Catholic Lawyers' Guilds, Rosary Societies, Holy Name Societies, the Knights of Columbus, Marriage Encounter Groups, the Christian Family Movement, Cana Conferences, Conferences of Religious Women and Religious Men, Councils and Senates of Priests as well as Ecumenical Groups. Now is the time for members of other religious faiths to speak to the Catholic Church about their teaching and law concerning the rights of persons to divorce and remarry.

Our Bishops must hear from single and married Catholics as well as divorced persons that they are concerned and distressed because of the injustice of the present Church law concerning divorce and remarriage. Catholics, whether or not they are personally afflicted by the problem, will vindicate the rights of divorced persons if they speak their convictions directly and openly to the Bishops.

MONSIGNOR STEPHEN J. KELLEHER, D.C.L.
Sacred Heart of Jesus Church
New York, New York